the **PASSPORT** PROGRAM

the **PASSPORT** PROGRAM

A Journey through
Emotional, Social,
Cognitive, and
Self-Development

GRADES
9-12

ANN VERNON

Research Press • 2612 North Mattis Avenue • Champaign, Illinois 61822
(800) 519-2707 • www.researchpress.com

CONTENTS

Grade 9

SELF-DEVELOPMENT

EMOTIONAL DEVELOPMENT

SOCIAL DEVELOPMENT

COGNITIVE DEVELOPMENT

Grade 10

SELF-DEVELOPMENT

Grade 11

Cognitive Development

ACTIVITY

Grade 12

Self-Development

ACTIVITY

Emotional Development

ACTIVITY

Social Development

ACTIVITY

Cognitive Development

ACTIVITY

HANDOUTS

Grade 9

Grade 10

Grade 11

Grade 12

FOREWORD

In the early 1970s, Rational-Emotive Education was a gleam in the eye of Albert Ellis. One of its earliest implementations was in the Living School, a pioneering school run by the Institute for Rational Living in New York City.

Since that time, giant leaps have been made by educators and mental health professionals in using rational thinking and emotional self-management skills to foster positive mental health in children and adolescents. Among the very richest and most creative contributions have been made by Ann Vernon, one of this country's outstanding counselor educators, whose two previous volumes of Rational-Emotive Education curricula are in wide use in schools and counseling offices throughout the U.S. and abroad.

In this important new work, Dr. Vernon brings her understanding of how to help youngsters become happy, self-accepting, and well-functioning adults into the future. Today's children face not only normal developmental problems, but also a myriad of potentially overwhelming stressors unimaginable in previous generations. As educators, parents, and mental health professionals, we will surely need all the resources we can muster to help safeguard our children from self-downing, irrational thinking, debilitating emotions, and self-defeating behaviors.

A unique aspect of this book is that it offers an array of vignettes of real-life issues applicable to youngsters of all cultural and socioeconomic backgrounds. Situations dealt with range from doing poorly on a test and handling unfairness and rejection through coping with disruptive family situations and being tempted by drug-experimenting peers. Dr. Vernon is superb at entering children's and adolescents' experiential worlds. Many of the vignettes in the series are eloquent first-person accounts by the youngsters themselves, talking about their struggles and how they were able to use rational thinking skills to help them increase self-acceptance, deal with troublesome emotions, and overcome self-defeating behaviors. Engaging "lessons"–adaptable for both classroom or counseling settings– each present a developmentally appropriate stimulus activity, skills for dealing with this stimulus, and follow-up questions and activities that allow youngsters to make the transition from intellectual insight to direct application of concepts and skills in their own lives.

This highly practical resource will be a great boon to all who wish to help grow a crop of children and adolescents who are secure in themselves and their values, resilient and flexible in dealing with life's stressors and challenges, and able to relate effectively and responsibly to others and pursue their dreams.

JANET L. WOLFE, PH.D.
EXECUTIVE DIRECTOR
ALBERT ELLIS INSTITUTE

ACKNOWLEDGMENTS

This book and its companion volumes for grades 1–5 and grades 6–8 are the result of a conviction that we cannot leave the challenges of growing up to chance. Rather, we need to teach children and adolescents systematically how to navigate each stage of development so that they don't give up before they grow up. In my estimation, there is no better way to do that than to teach young people how to apply the principles of Rational-Emotive Behavior Therapy to the problems of growing up. I have been using REBT with children and adolescents for many years and want to acknowledge Albert Ellis, Janet Wolfe, Ray DiGiuseppe, and Dominic DiMattia for sharing their knowledge and expertise with me and for supporting my efforts to apply these concepts in educational settings.

I want to thank my colleague David Martino for his thorough review and critique of my material. In addition, appreciation goes to the school counselors, many of whom are my former students, who piloted these materials and offered helpful suggestions.

A big thank-you goes to the Research Press staff—Ann Wendel, Russ Pence, and Karen Steiner—for enthusiastically endorsing this project and supporting me throughout the process with their helpful suggestions. It is indeed a pleasure to work with them.

Last but not least, I want to express appreciation to the parents of my clients, who trusted me with the privilege of working with their children and adolescents in my private counseling practice. My utmost gratitude goes to the young people who have been my clients. Many of the ideas in these volumes originated from work I did with them. The lessons they have taught me have been invaluable, and it has been gratifying to see how they can think, feel, and behave in healthier ways as a result of intervention. The stories in the first volume are all based on actual experiences young people shared with me. The stories and poems in the two companion volumes, including this one, are all written by adolescents, who hoped that "telling their stories" would help other kids their age through the developmental process.

INTRODUCTION: THE DEVELOPMENTAL PERSPECTIVE

That was then; this is now. Some things change, and some things stay the same. These two phrases accurately describe some of what I think about when I reflect on child and adolescent development. In some ways, being a young person today is significantly different than it was when many of us were growing up. Back then, we used drugs if we had physical illness. Now many young people use drugs to numb their emotional pain. Back then, violence was something that occasionally happened in big cities. Now violence is every-where and has a tremendous impact on the lives of children and adolescents. Back then, child and adolescent depression was rare. Now it is almost an epidemic. Back then, most families were like the Cleavers in *Leave It to Beaver*. Now most children grow up in dual-worker families, and many of them at some point in their lives live in single-parent or blended family structures. Back then, we rarely heard about child or adolescent suicide. Now it is the second leading cause of death among adolescents.

These comparisons could go on and on. In some ways, life for children and adolescents is very different, and in other ways, many of the issues are the same. I recall a discussion with my son the summer after his senior year in high school. He was complaining about having to go to Wisconsin for a family vacation. "Mom, you just don't understand. I want to stay home with my friends because it's my last summer and my friends are really important to me. I don't want to miss out on everything by being gone." He seemed convinced that I wouldn't understand, but his statements brought back a flood of memories. Without saying a word, I went to my file and pulled out a letter I had written to my mother the summer after my senior year in high school, when we were having a discussion about going to our cabin. I handed it to Eric. "Dear Mom," the letter read. "I just have to stay home this summer. You know there is nothing for me to do at the cabin. You probably can't imagine it, but kids my age want action. We can't help it; that's just the way we are. I've got to be with my friends. Please don't make me go."

After that, nothing more was said. Eric, his father, and I negotiated the amount of time Eric would be gone, and I don't imagine he really missed out on any more than I did by being "away from the action" for a few days. But of course neither one of us saw it that way when we were 18 years old. This is just one example of how some things stay the same, and as I listen to children and adolescents express their thoughts and feelings to me in counseling sessions, I am repeatedly reminded of the fact that developmental stages have remained relatively constant.

It is imperative that we know about developmental stages and characteristics. Without understanding what growing up is all about, we run the risk of overreacting or underreacting to problematic symptoms; we may not see a situation for what it truly is. This point hit home for me when I was listening to an audiotape presented by one of my practicum students. My student believed her client might be in an abusive relationship with her mother. "Let's listen to the tape," I said to my student. And as I listened, I heard a 15-year-old young woman describing her conflictual relationship with her mother. She spoke about how her mother never let her do anything, was always yelling at her, and was continually making her do things she didn't want to do. I asked my student if she had probed for specific examples, explaining that it is very characteristic for young adolescents to overgeneralize and approach everything dichotomously: Either they get to do everything, or they get to do nothing, for example. I certainly did not want to imply that an abusive relationship was out of the question in this case, but I cautioned my student to look at the problem through multiple lenses, to ask for specific examples, and to take into account what we know about adolescent females—that many have love-hate relationships with their mothers, that they usually feel oppressed, and that they generally don't want to be forced to do anything they don't want to because this thwarts their growing need for independence. My student went back to her counselee, armed with new perspectives. Over the course of several sessions, including an interview with the client and her mother, it became apparent that this case exemplified typical adolescent issues, not an abusive relationship.

Developmental characteristics not only need to be taken into account when we assess problems, they also need to be considered as we look at how young people interpret events. One third grader wrote a will to designate which friends would get his prized possessions in case something happened to him. His parents were understandably concerned, thinking their son might be contemplating suicide. As it turned out, he wrote a will because his teacher had been sharing a current event about children who had been trapped in a cave. This youngster assumed that if something like that could happen to other children, it might happen to him, and he wanted to make sure his friends received his favorite things. Younger children interpret things very literally because they are concrete thinkers. In this case, cognitive development limited the way the child interpreted his situation, and these limitations in turn influenced his behavior. We must also remember that despite the fact that developmental stages and characteristics haven't changed much over the decades, change has occurred in the cultural and social factors that affect the lives of young people. Children in today's society grow up faster. As Mary Pipher, author of *Reviving Ophelia*, notes, "The protected place in space and time that we once called childhood has grown shorter" (1994, p. 28). Now, in addition to dealing with typical growing-up issues, which in themselves can be challenging and confusing, children and adolescents have much more to cope with. Many grow up in poverty, are victims of abuse, or struggle with parental divorce or remarriage. Superimpose these problems on top of the normal growing-up problems, and it is no wonder that far too many young people deal with their issues in unhealthy ways. In part, unhealthy responses also reflect developmental capabilities. For young adolescents, whose sense of time is the here and now and whose thinking is still for the most part concrete, numbing pain with drugs and alcohol seems like the easiest thing to do when life becomes overwhelming. They simply do not have the ability to consider consequences carefully.

The frightening aspect of how children and adolescents cope with developmental as well as situational problems is that long-term consequences may have a profoundly negative impact on their lives. But because they live in the present and aren't able to project far into the future, many young people deal with these stressors as best they can given their levels of development. In other words, if they don't have the ability to take other perspectives or see alternatives, it is often difficult for them to use the good judgment we as adults think they should be capable of employing. We need to remember that young people interpret their world differently than we do.

Although many young people are able to meet the challenges of growing up, we can probably remember from our own experience wondering if we were "normal"–if what was happening to us was typical. I see my clients breathe sighs of relief when I reassure them that they are normal and help them understand why they are thinking, feeling, and behaving as they are, given their levels of development. It seems to me that we take too much for granted, assuming that young people somehow know what is normal, when in fact they have no clue. This assumption creates anxiety and confusion. If this fear is not addressed, it can compound other problems, and young people can become overwhelmed and discouraged. This is the point at which we most need to intervene.

An Emotional Health Curriculum

This volume in *The Passport Program* series gives educators and mental health professionals a comprehensive curriculum to help young people in mid-adolescence learn positive mental health concepts and navigate the journey through the situational and developmental problems of growing up. This book presents 64 activities, field tested with adolescents in grades 9–12. These activities are designed not only to teach young people what is normal but also to help them learn effective strategies for dealing with problems characteristic of their age group. Organized by grade level, the activities cover four key areas: Self-Development, Emotional Development, Social Development, and Cognitive Development.

The activities are sequential and, if used with the companion volumes for middle childhood and early adolescence, provide a comprehensive developmental curriculum for grades 1–12. Each activity includes a short statement about developmental perspective, specific objectives, a step-by-step lesson, and content and personalization questions. Content questions relate directly to the content of the stimulus activity and are designed to ensure mastery of concepts and processing of the stimulus activity. Personalization questions encourage young people to apply the concepts to their own lives. These questions move them from intellectualizing about what they have learned to integrating the concepts personally. At the center of each activity is a creative, developmentally appropriate stimulus procedure that addresses the objectives and provides an opportunity for young people to learn more about developmental issues typical for their age group, as well as to master skills for dealing with these issues. At the end is a follow-up activity, which reinforces the concepts in a variety of ways, including actual skill practice.

Theoretical Foundations

An important feature of this curriculum is that it is strongly grounded in developmental theory, as well as in principles of Rational-Emotive Behavior Therapy. An overview of these theories follows, but readers are encouraged to study further by consulting the references and suggested readings at the end of this introduction.

Developmental Characteristics: Mid-Adolescence

During mid-adolescence, ages 15–18, teenagers have a growing need for independence. The emotional upheaval of early adolescence has generally lost some of its intensity, depending on the age at which the young person entered puberty. In addition, adolescents at this point are more likely to have developed abstract thinking skills, which enable them to reason and use better problem-solving skills. However, these cognitive abilities also depend on individual level of development.

During this period, adolescents are often less confident than they care to admit. They may bolster their confidence through rebellion or defiance, usually in direct correlation with their desire to prove they are independent. This is a time when young people try on adult roles. In addition to achieving an identity that is integrated and unique, the adolescent must acquire a new status in the family, as relationships with parents take on a different form, and must move toward an autonomous position in relation to the larger world, particularly in terms of career development. Peer relationships also change as young people become more secure and no longer need to be carbon copies of their peers, as they did in early adolescence. Friendships during mid-adolescence continue to be an important source of identity and value development, and intimate friendships with peers of both the same and the opposite gender increase during this time.

As previously noted, adolescents by this time are generally less volatile, less egocentric, and increasingly able to think more abstractly. For the most part, they are more introspective, and their thought processes are more flexible. They are less likely to think in either-or terms, and their increased ability to see the complexity of situations has a positive impact on their ability to problem solve. All of these factors are crucial during a time when young people must begin to make important decisions about the future and deal with more complex moral dilemmas.

Principles of Rational-Emotive Behavior Therapy

Rational-Emotive Behavior Therapy (REBT), developed by Albert Ellis (Ellis, 1994; Ellis & Dryden, 1997), is based on the assumption that what we think directly determines how we feel and behave. Ellis created the A-B-C model of emotional disturbance to explain the relationship between activating events *(A's),* beliefs *(B's),* and emotional and behavioral consequences *(C's).* According to this theory, the activating event does not create emotional upset since two people can experience the same event and react to it differently. Rather, what one thinks about the event results in the emotional and behavioral reactions. Ellis maintains that disturbed, negative emotions are caused by absolutistic, rigid, and demanding thoughts that he labeled as *irrational.* Irrational beliefs fall into three major categories: *shoulds, musts,* and *oughts,* which reflect unrealistic demands on people or situations; *evaluations of worth,* which relate to having to do well and win approval in order to consider oneself a worthwhile person; and *need statements,* which reflect what one thinks one must have to be comfortable and free of frustration. For children and adolescents, the *shoulds, musts,* and *oughts* translate into expectations: I should always get to do what I want, people should treat me exactly as I think they should treat me, and everything in life should always be fair. *Evaluations of worth* translate into judgmental statements: I must be perfect; I can't make mistakes; if others reject me or I don't do well, I am a worthless kid. *Need statements* reflect young people's irrational belief that everything in life should be easy: I shouldn't have to work too hard at anything or do things that are boring, and I can't stand discomfort. These irrational beliefs result in intense negative emotions, which prevent children and adolescents from engaging in effective problem solving.

For psychological health, these irrational beliefs must be replaced with *rational* beliefs. Rational beliefs result in moderate, less disturbed emotions; are based on reality; and help one achieve one's goals. The process by which rational beliefs are identified is called *disputing (D).* Disputing involves a variety of techniques for changing thinking, feeling, and behaving. Specifically, the main disputational methods include detecting illogical and unrealistic beliefs by asking questions designed to challenge these thoughts, using rational-emotive imagery, and using self-talk and self-dialogues. In addition, behavioral methods such as reinforcement, skill training, and homework assignments are widely employed.

Once irrational beliefs have been identified, the result is a reduction in the disturbing emotion. This is not to say that one goes from feeling depressed to happy, or angry to slightly irritated. However, the intensity of the emotion is reduced as illogical, irrational beliefs are replaced by more sensible thoughts. For example, if a teenager didn't get invited to a party and irrationally thought that no one liked her, that she would never have friends again, or that she was worthless because she had been rejected, she might feel very sad. If she realized through disputation that she was still a worthwhile kid even if she hadn't been invited to this party and that there was no evidence to support the notion that no one liked her or that she would never have friends again, she would still feel some sadness, but it would not be as intense. And, whereas she might have moped around for days when she was feeling intensely sad, she might be able to entertain herself in other ways and find some pleasure in doing those things if she were not as sad. The final stages of the model, therefore, are the *E* (effective new philosophy) and the *F* (new feeling).

REBT has a long history of use with children and adolescents in educational as well as therapeutic settings. The principles can be readily adapted for younger populations and have been applied to a wide variety of problems. Ellis, a long-time proponent of the use of REBT in educational settings, stresses the importance of a prevention curriculum designed to help young people help themselves by learning positive mental health concepts. Rational-Emotive Education, or REE, is a systematic curricular approach to emotional education in which planned, sequential lessons are presented. The major goal of REE is to teach rational thinking skills so young people may more effectively solve problems, gain emotional insight, and learn sensible coping strategies to minimize emotional distress commonly experienced in childhood and adolescence. The ultimate goal of a curriculum of this nature is to help young people get better, not just feel better, and to provide them with the emotional and behavioral tools to deal more effectively with present and future problems. The activities presented in this volume are based on fundamental principles of REE and stress the application of these concepts to developmental problems.

Using Program Materials

Given the fact that growing up is more difficult than ever before, the importance of a prevention curriculum cannot be overstressed. Preventive mental health programs facilitate all aspects of development and help young people develop self-acceptance, good interpersonal relationship skills, problem-solving and decision-making strategies, skills to deal with troublesome emotions, and a more flexible outlook on life. If used intentionally and sequentially, these programs can provide adolescents with information and skills that will certainly not eliminate all problems but can minimize the intensity, severity, and duration of problems.

The activities in this book are intended to be used primarily in classroom or small-group counseling settings. With minor changes, they can also be used in individual counseling in school or mental health settings. The developmental concepts are applicable to all teenagers, but the process or the activity may need to be adapted for specific populations. The questions at the end of each activity are designed to stimulate discussion, and leaders are expected to expand or modify them according to the needs of the individual or group.

The stimulus activities are designed to last 20–30 minutes and to be followed by discussion. Obviously, this time will vary depending on the group. Some lessons may need to be divided so that the activity is completed one day, with discussion following the next. Discussion is a critical part of these lessons because it reinforces objectives and allows young people to apply the concepts to their own lives. Since many of the activities encourage self-disclosure, it is vital to establish an atmosphere of trust and cohesiveness before implementing the program. Although most of the activities are relatively nonthreatening, teenagers must have the right to "pass" if they are uncomfortable with the discussion. Just hearing other participants share and discuss will help normalize their feelings, and they will learn from the experience. Establishing ground rules can help ensure that young people respect one another's opinions and expressions. They need to understand that these discussions are confidential and should stay within the group, that they have a right to pass, and that there should be no put-downs. Ground rules help provide a safe place for them to learn and apply these mental health principles.

As educators and mental health practitioners, we need to do what we can to safeguard children and adolescents against self-deprecation, irrational thinking, debilitating emotions, and self-defeating behaviors. We need to help them build resilience by teaching them how to think, feel, and behave in healthy ways. Giving them these tools should be an educational priority: It is far easier to prevent problems than to deal with them after the fact. Implementing this curriculum is a step toward facilitating young people's self-, social, emotional, and cognitive development.

References and Suggested Reading

DiGiuseppe, R., & Bernard, M. (1990). The application of rational-emotive theory and therapy to school-aged children. *School Psychology Review, 19,* 287–293.

Dryden, W., & DiGiuseppe, R. (1990). *A primer on Rational-Emotive Therapy.* Champaign, IL: Research Press.

Elkind, D. (1988). *The hurried child.* Reading, MA: Addison-Wesley.

Ellis, A. (1994). *Reason and emotion in psychotherapy.* New York: Carol.

Ellis, A., & Dryden, W. (1997). *The practice of REBT.* New York: Springer.

Pipher, M. (1994). *Reviving Ophelia: Saving the selves of adolescent girls.* New York: Ballantine.

Vernon, A. (1993). *Developmental assessment and intervention with children and adolescents.* Alexandria, VA: American Counseling Association.

Vernon, A., & Al-Mabuk, R. (1995). *What growing up is all about: A parent's guide to child and adolescent development.* Champaign, IL: Research Press.

Walen, S., DiGiuseppe, R., & Dryden, W. (1992). *A practitioner's guide to Rational-Emotive Therapy.* New York: Oxford University Press.

Wilde, J. (1992). *Rational counseling with school-aged populations: A practical guide.* Muncie, IN: Accelerated Development.

the **PASSPORT** PROGRAM

GRADE 9

Self-Development
ACTIVITY
1   Pieces of the Puzzle
2   What's Important to Me?
3   I'm Invincible
4   What Does It Mean about Me?

Emotional Development
ACTIVITY
1   Agreeable to Argumentative
2   Mood Management
3   The Emotional Roller Coaster
4   Anger Is . . .

Social Development
ACTIVITY
1   Fights with Friends
2   Rational Relationships
3   Peers and Pressure
4   Feedback from Friends

Cognitive Development
ACTIVITY
1   Think, Feel, Do
2   Awesome Outcome
3   Problem-Solving Skills
4   Realistic Reasoning

Pieces of the Puzzle

Developmental Perspective

Identity development continues to be a major issue for 15- to 18-year-olds. The process of finding oneself at this age involves establishing sexual, vocational, social, moral, political, and religious identity. Adolescents do this by trying on various roles and responsibilities, engaging in discussions, observing peers and adults, and doing a great deal of self-questioning, experimenting, and exploring.

Objective

▷ To learn more about one's identity

Materials

▷ A small manila envelope containing Pieces of the Puzzle–Cards (Handout 1) for each student

▷ Paper and pencil for each student

Procedure

1. Introduce the lesson by discussing the fact that piecing together one's identity is a major task during adolescence and that this can sometimes be a puzzling process. Ask students to take out paper and pencil and respond to the following:

   ► Do you feel you know more about yourself now than you did five years ago? If so, how has this happened?

   ► Do you ever feel confused about who you are relative to certain aspects of your feelings, behaviors, or beliefs?

   ► Do you think your view of yourself will continue to change in the next five years?

   ► Do you think you know yourself well or not very well?

   Invite students to share their responses with partners.

2. Distribute the envelopes containing the Pieces of the Puzzle–Cards (Handout 1). Ask each student to write on each piece at least two or three words describing who he or she is relative to the category identified on the puzzle piece.

3. Allow time for students to put their puzzles together and share their results in triads. Invite sharing with the total group.

4. Discuss the Content and Personalization Questions.

Discussion

CONTENT QUESTIONS

1. Was it difficult to think about how to describe yourself in these different categories? Were some categories more difficult for you than others? If so, which ones?

2. On the basis of your responses to the puzzle, how are you like or unlike the other people in your small group? (Invite sharing of similarities and differences.)

PERSONALIZATION QUESTIONS

1. What did you learn about yourself by doing the puzzle?

2. In what areas are you still trying to figure out who you are?

3. How do you think your identity might change in the next four years?

Follow-up Activity

Have each student take one or two of the puzzle categories and design a collage that depicts who he or she is in the specific area(s).

Pieces of the Puzzle

CARDS

Leader note: Copy and cut apart; give one set to each student.

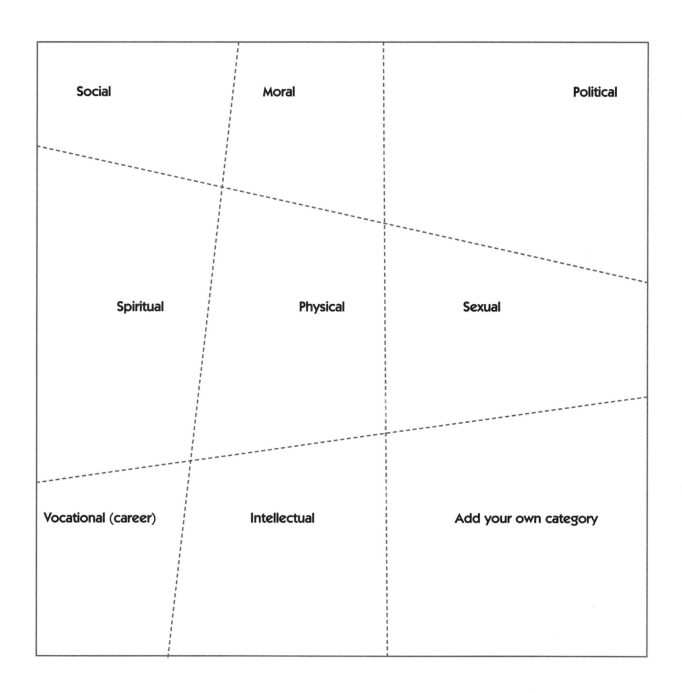

Social	Moral	Political
Spiritual	Physical	Sexual
Vocational (career)	Intellectual	Add your own category

What's Important to Me?

Developmental Perspective

As adolescents pursue the quest for identity, they continually engage in the process of clarifying what's important to them. Because peer influence is so strong at this stage of development, it is particularly critical for young people to clarify their own values and beliefs so they won't be negatively influenced by peers.

Objective

▷ To clarify values and beliefs

Materials

▷ A copy of the What's Important to Me? Rank-Order Worksheet (Handout 2) and a pencil for each student

Procedure

1. Introduce the lesson by asking students to share examples of things they value or important beliefs they hold. Indicate that during adolescence these beliefs and values are sometimes challenged as a result of peer pressure, a desire to experiment, or an impulse to react against parents or other adults. The purpose of this lesson is to help them clarify values and beliefs.

2. Distribute a What's Important to Me? Rank-Order Worksheet (Handout 2) to each student. Instruct students to rank order the items from most to least important depending on their values.

3. After students have completed the rankings, break them into groups of four to discuss their results.

4. Discuss the Content and Personalization Questions.

Discussion

CONTENT QUESTIONS

1. How difficult was it for you to rank the items in the list?
2. What process did you use to make your ranking decisions?
3. How did you feel about sharing your rankings with others?
4. Were your rankings very similar or dissimilar to those of others in your group?
5. Were you surprised at how high or low you ranked certain items? (Encourage discussion about this.)

PERSONALIZATION QUESTIONS

1. How do you act on what's important to you?

2. Do you ever choose to compromise what's important to you? If so, under what conditions do you do this?

3. Do you think that what's important will change as you get older? For example, would your rankings have been the same if you had done them last year?

4. What did you learn about yourself from this activity?

Follow-up Activity

Have students design their own rank orders involving additional issues relevant to them. Invite them to present the results to partners and have the partners rank the items.

What's Important to Me?

RANK-ORDER WORKSHEET

Name: _____ Date: _____

Instructions: Read the 15 items on the list, and rank them according to the degree of importance to you (1 = most important, 15 = least important).

_____ Being nonviolent

_____ Going to church/practicing my religion

_____ Doing well in sports, music, or drama

_____ Spending time with my friends

_____ My reputation

_____ Being part of a group

_____ Having freedom to do what I want

_____ Staying drug and alcohol free

_____ Racial equality

_____ Money

_____ Equality for males and females

_____ Doing well in school

_____ Being popular

_____ My relationship with my parents

_____ Having a boyfriend or a girlfriend

I'm Invincible

Developmental Perspective

Adolescents feel unique and are egocentric. This fact has some negative implications. In particular, they believe that because they are special, bad things may happen to others but not to them. In other words, they think they can use drugs or alcohol and not become addicted or can be sexually active and not get pregnant. An important aspect of their development is to help them overcome this sense of invincibility so they can look realistically at consequences.

Objectives

▷ To learn that one is not invincible

▷ To identify consequences of believing that one is invincible

Materials

▷ A copy of the I'm Invincible–Story (Handout 3) for each student

Procedure

1. Introduce the activity by briefly discussing the concepts outlined in the Developmental Perspective. Ask students to share examples of behavior they consider to be related to feeling invincible.

2. Distribute the I'm Invincible–Story (Handout 3) to each student. Explain that it is the true story of an 18-year-old's experience with alcohol. After students have had time to read the story, have them discuss their reactions to the story with partners.

3. Discuss the Content and Personalization Questions.

Discussion

CONTENT QUESTIONS

1. Do you think the teenager in the story was aware of what could happen before she drank that amount of alcohol? Do you think her friends realized what was happening?

2. Do you know teenagers who have had similar experiences? If so, how did the experience affect them?

3. What are the long-term consequences for the teenager in the story?

4. Do you think there are always consequences when teenagers do things because they think they are invincible?

PERSONALIZATION QUESTIONS

1. Have you ever been in a situation where you thought something bad could happen to others but not to you? (Invite sharing.)

2. Do you think about consequences–about what might happen to you–or do you ignore them because you think you are invincible?

3. Did you learn anything from this lesson that might affect your behavior in the future?

Follow-up Activity

Invite several older students to participate in a panel discussion about the importance of looking at the bigger picture and not assuming that they are immune from bad things happening to them.

I'm Invincible

STORY—PAGE 1

Up until seventh grade, I was a pretty normal kid. I had good friends, got decent grades, and got along well with my parents. But by the end of seventh grade, I started hanging out with different friends because my closest friend had moved away and the others were getting snotty. The new group I was with was a lot different from my old friends, and they all decided to try drinking. I'm not sure exactly how old I was when I started, but I remember that I had just turned 14 when I got drunk for the first time. After that I started drinking pretty regularly on the weekends.

During the second semester of eighth grade, my grades really went down. I got kicked out of classes and activities and was in quite a bit of trouble at school. My parents were really strict, so I was grounded a lot. They were on my case all the time. But that didn't stop me. I started drinking more, and by the summer after eighth grade I was drinking a lot. It was something to do with my friends when we were bored, and because we hung out with older kids, it was easy to get. Once in a while I would refuse to drink, but not very often because I thought it was fun, and I didn't have to worry about things if I was drunk.

During my freshman year I continued to drink, but my tolerance level had increased, so it took more to get drunk. That's when I started smoking pot—I only did it a few times and didn't really get into it. My grades were really bad, and I was in constant trouble at school and at home. My parents suspected that I drank, but I didn't think about stopping. It seemed normal since all my friends were doing it. People thought it was cool that I could drink a lot—actually more than guys who were a lot older than me. I could chug at least eight beers, one after the other, and only get a little buzz. Because it took more for me to get drunk, I kept increasing the amount I drank.

My parents finally made me go to an outpatient alcohol rehabilitation program for a month, but it didn't do any good. I didn't want to be there because I didn't really think I had a problem. My parents were angry that I thought treatment was such a joke, and they grounded me for the rest of the school year.

Two weeks after school ended my freshman year, I finally was able to go out. I went to a friend's house for the afternoon. We didn't have anything to do, so we started drinking. I remember drinking a lot of hard liquor and lying down, and the next thing I knew I woke up in the hospital. I had overdosed. I don't remember much about what happened after I went to my friend's house. Apparently we were all drunk, and my friends were passing out and throwing up blood. One of their boyfriends came over and tried to get me up. Nothing worked, so he called the ambulance.

I'm Invincible

STORY—PAGE 2

On the way to the hospital I almost died, and they had to airlift me from that hospital to another one. I was there for about a week, and then my parents took me on a long vacation to get me away from all the rumors and from the friends who had been with me that afternoon. The whole summer I hardly left the house because I was so embarrassed. My friends basically ignored me.

When school started, I went back but it was awful. I was really ashamed. I lived in a small town, so everyone knew what had happened. People pretty much ignored me. I thought everyone was talking about me, even though they probably weren't, at least as much as I thought they were. My grades were better for a while, but then I got really depressed. I essentially had no life; my parents wouldn't let me go anywhere because they were afraid I'd drink again and overdose. Even though I was about to turn 16, they wouldn't let me get my license because they were afraid of what I'd do if I had more freedom to come and go.

Right after the second semester started, I dropped out of school. I just couldn't stand it any longer. People were always making comments about me, including the teachers, and I was getting more and more depressed. I was hospitalized for depression and was there a week. It didn't do any good, so I went to another hospital, and that was worse. Then my parents sent me to a drug rehabilitation center. It was better than the other hospitals, and I learned a lot about my tolerance level. But I still wasn't ready to admit that I had a problem with drinking. Because I wasn't really working the program, they sent me home.

I was still very depressed, suicidal, and very anxious. I was paranoid about seeing people in town because I knew they were talking about me and didn't like me. I seldom left the house. Things got worse, and I was hospitalized again for a month. They changed my medication, but that didn't help much. After I was released, I went home for a few months, but I was still so depressed that I'm not sure why I even stayed alive. My parents put me back in another hospital, and this time they doped me up on so many meds that my blood pressure was dangerously low. Because my parents were so upset with the doctors, they arranged to transfer me to another hospital. I was sick of hospitals because nobody was able to help me. I was so desperate about not going that when my mother stopped to get something to eat, I took the car and left. Finally I realized I had no idea where I was going or what I would do, so I went back and got my mother and checked into the new hospital. They got me off the bad meds and I finally felt better.

I'm Invincible

STORY—PAGE 3

All during this time I was very angry, defiant, depressed, and anxious. I developed obsessive-compulsive disorder and constantly needed reassurance from my parents that people didn't hate me. I was really dependent on them because I couldn't function very well on my own, and I hated that. I had no life. I was at home with them 24 hours a day. Occasionally one of my friends and her boyfriend would come over or call, but other than that, no one paid attention to me. I was afraid to go places because of what people would say.

The new medication finally started to work, and I was in counseling, too. I slowly started to get better and wanted to get out more. I started studying for my GED and passed all the course work, so by the end of my junior year I had completed high school. I enrolled in a community college and started taking courses there this year. I am going out more and am not nearly as anxious. Even though I'm a lot better, I went through hell for about two years. I certainly didn't have a normal high school life.

I have a lot of regrets. I wish I'd stayed in school, but because of what I'd done, I just couldn't take it. I wish I could undo the day I overdosed, but I can't. It wrecked my life for a long time, and it's still not what most kids would consider normal. My parents still don't trust me, so I have a curfew and have to check in with them all the time. At times I'd like to move into my own apartment, but I can't get a job, so I don't have any money. There are still people who avoid me; I don't have a lot of friends.

Because of the amount of alcohol I consumed, it ate the lining of my stomach, so I have a hard time digesting food. I also have some long-term memory loss, so learning is harder for me. The doctors aren't sure how much brain damage there was, but they said that it is impossible to drink as much as I did and be in a coma for eight hours and not have some damage. I had no idea what I was doing when I started drinking and didn't think that bad things would happen to me if I drank that much. It was just something to do.

But bad things did happen. If my friend's boyfriend hadn't come when he did, I would have died. And sometimes I've wished I had because life has never been the same since. I can't change what happened, but I hope that others will think about what could happen and drink more responsibly than I did if they choose to drink.

–Jessica, Age 18

What Does It Mean about Me?

Developmental Perspective

At this stage of development, adolescents are beginning to think more abstractly. However, the rate at which these thinking skills develop varies a great deal, and many adolescents still react personally to feedback, criticism, or failure, tending to equate who they are with what they do. This tendency to personalize can have a very negative impact on self-concept as well as on emotional well-being.

Objective

▷ To learn that performance in one area is not a reflection of one's total worth as a person

Materials

▷ A copy of the What Does It Mean about Me? Game Board (Handout 4) and a set of What Does It Mean about Me? Game Cards (Handout 5) for every group of three students

▷ A pencil for each student

Procedure

1. Discuss the concept of equating self-worth with performance in one area, using the following example to illustrate the point:

   You are riding in a car. The car is several years old, but it is still in very good shape. Suddenly the tire goes flat. Do you get rid of the car because it's a piece of junk, or do you realize that the car is still fine, that it just has a flat tire?

   Most people would realize that the car is still in good shape, but that it has one flat tire that needs to be fixed. This is how human beings are. For example, someone might perform poorly on a test, but that doesn't mean she is a stupid person. Or someone may have a bad soccer game, but that doesn't mean he is a bad soccer player. The danger of equating performance at one point in time with self-worth is that if you continually get down on yourself, it is easy to give up and think that nothing you do matters. When this happens over and over, it is easy to get down on yourself.

2. Divide students into triads and distribute the What Does It Mean about Me? Game Boards (Handout 4) and Game Cards (Handout 5).

3. Allow sufficient time for students to play the game, and then discuss the Content and Personalization Questions.

Discussion

CONTENT QUESTIONS

1. Was it difficult to figure out which responses did not equate self-worth with performance?

2. What do you see as the danger of taking feedback, criticism, or poor performance so personally that you think you are a bad person?

PERSONALIZATION QUESTIONS

1. Have you ever equated your self-worth with your performance? If so, was this a good thing for you?

2. If you have a tendency to equate your self-worth with your performance, is this something you want to change? If so, what do you think you can do to change this pattern?

3. What did you learn from this lesson that may be helpful to you?

Follow-up Activity

Have students work in small groups to generate their own examples of situations and ways of thinking similar to the examples given in the activity. Allow them to play the game again using the new examples.

What Does It Mean about Me?

GAME BOARD

*Instructions: Work in groups of three. One person in the group will be the scorekeeper.
The scorekeeper will not play the game but will look up the correct response to each
question. The other two players will take turns drawing a card and trying to identify the
response that does not equate self-worth as a person with performance in one area or at
one point in time. When a player states a response (A or B), the scorekeeper looks up
the answer. If the answer is correct, the player chooses X or O and marks the board as in
tic-tac-toe. The first person to mark three in a row (horizontally, vertically, or diagonally)
wins the game.*

What Does It Mean about Me?

GAME CARDS—PAGE 1

Leader note: Copy and cut apart; give one set to each group of three students. Give the scorekeeper the Answer Sheet.

1. You just got back results from a science test. You usually get 98 to 100 percent, but on this test you got a 92. You think:

   A. I'm an idiot. The questions I missed were bogus questions. Now I'll get a *B* in this course for sure.

   B. I wish I'd done better. The questions I missed were pretty simple. I'll have to try harder next time to bring my grade up.

2. You have to give a speech tomorrow. You think:

   A. I'm nervous. I hate giving speeches. It feels like everyone is looking at me.

   B. I hate giving speeches. I know I'll screw up. Then everyone will laugh and think I'm really dumb, which I will be if I don't do it right.

3. You are the lead three-point shooter on the basketball team. At last night's game you were cold. You missed all but one of your three-point shots. You think:

   A. It's because of me that we lost the game. I'm a terrible player.

   B. So I had a bad night. That doesn't mean I'm not a good player most of the time.

4. You've got the lead role in the school play. It's opening night, and you miss several of your lines. You think:

   A. How could I be so stupid? I looked like a fool in front of everyone. I might as well forget about my chances of getting another lead role since I'm such a terrible actor.

   B. How could I have missed those lines? I knew them before tonight. I guess a few others missed some, too; I just hope it doesn't ruin my chances for another lead role.

5. You hear about a party that you weren't invited to. You think:

   A. I wonder why they didn't invite me, but I guess I can't expect everyone to like me.

   B. They don't like me. I must have done something to turn them against me. Why am I such a loser?

6. You applied for a baby-sitting job for the summer. You didn't get it. You think:

   A. They probably didn't ask me because they didn't think I could handle the responsibility. I'm no good at anything.

   B. I wish I'd gotten the job, but it doesn't mean that I can't do anything right or that I couldn't have handled this responsibility.

What Does It Mean about Me?

GAME CARDS–PAGE 2

7. You get an *F* on your report card. The rest of the grades are *B's* and *C's*. You think:

    A. Just because I got the one *F*, it doesn't mean I'm a stupid kid or no good at anything.

    B. I'm stupid; I'll flunk ninth grade.

8. You didn't get selected for the first chair in orchestra. You think:

    A. I'm a rotten viola player. All that practicing was for nothing. I might as well quit.

    B. I wish I'd made first chair, but it doesn't mean I'm a rotten player. I'll just have to practice harder if I want to move up from second chair.

9. Your boyfriend or girlfriend drops you and starts going out with someone else. You think:

    A. I don't understand what happened. I hope it's not something I did. But it doesn't mean that I'm a terrible person or that I'll never have another date again.

    B. I'm ugly, stupid, and no good. No one will ever want to go out with me again.

10. You broke your curfew and stayed out several hours later than you should have last night. Your father had no idea where you were. When you got home, he was relieved but told you he thought you'd probably been in a car accident. You think:

    A. I'm totally irresponsible. I always screw up. I didn't think he'd be so worried. Why can't I be a perfect kid like my brother?

    B. I guess I need to pay more attention to the time and call so he won't be so worried. I am responsible in other ways, so it doesn't mean I'm a total no-good.

Answer Sheet

1. B	6. B
2. A	7. A
3. B	8. B
4. B	9. A
5. A	10. B

Agreeable to Argumentative

Developmental Perspective

Within a matter of minutes, an adolescent can switch from being very agreeable to being very argumentative. These sudden mood shifts are confusing to the young person as well as to parents and teachers. Although it is normal for adolescents to experience these emotional and behavioral swings, it is also important to help them learn to put issues into perspective and understand that there are multiple points along the agreeable-to-argumentative continuum.

Objectives

▷ To understand the concept of a continuum of emotions

▷ To understand how to change feelings by changing thoughts

Materials

▷ A chalkboard

▷ A copy of the Agreeable to Argumentative–Discussion (Handout 6) for each group of three or four students

▷ Paper and pencil for each student

Procedure

1. To introduce the activity, draw a horizontal line across the board, and write the words *agreeable* at one end and *argumentative* at the other end. Explain the idea of a continuum of feelings. Note that there are many points between these extremes but that at this age, it is very common for young people to see only the extremes. Discuss the fact that seeing multiple points along the continuum helps a person manage feelings, thoughts, and behaviors.

2. Ask each student to take out paper and pencil and brainstorm at least 10 feeling words. Then have each one draw four horizontal lines across the page. Next, ask each student to think of two extremes of four of the identified emotions (one set per line) and write each set of extremes at either end of a continuum (for example, devastated/disappointed; elated/depressed).

3. Have students go back to the extremes on the continuum lines, identify four words that would describe in-between points on each line, and write those words on the appropriate lines.

4. Have students form groups of three or four to share their continuums. Following a short sharing period, distribute the Agreeable to Argumentative–Discussion (Handout 6). Have students read the handout and do the short exercises in their small groups.

5. Discuss the Content and Personalization Questions.

Discussion

CONTENT QUESTIONS

1. Was it difficult to identify several in-between points along your feeling continuums? Were some sets of words more difficult than others?

2. If you experience emotional extremes, how can changing your thoughts help you move more toward the center of a feeling continuum?

PERSONALIZATION QUESTIONS

1. Have you ever been able to move off either end of an emotional continuum? If so, how did you do it?

2. How do you think that changing your feelings by changing your thoughts will work for you?

3. What did you learn from this activity that might help you manage your emotional extremes more effectively?

Follow-up Activity

Ask each student to identify his or her emotional extremes for one day and to identify all the points along a continuum. Have students practice changing their thoughts to see if they can change their feelings.

Agreeable to Argumentative

DISCUSSION—PAGE 1

Instructions: Read the following information. Then do the exercises at the end.

There are many different ways to feel. Sometimes, however, it seems like there are only two feelings, which are the extreme opposites of each other. For example, has this ever happened to you? One minute you're sitting in the living room watching television with your parents, feeling very agreeable, and the next minute, someone says something that ticks you off just a little bit, and suddenly you are very argumentative. This is typical during adolescence, and it can be very confusing. Or, how about this experience? You've been feeling pretty happy and carefree, when suddenly you find yourself in a near panic about something. Sometimes these extremes don't feel very good, but what can you do about them? One thing you can do is understand the connection between how you think and how you feel. This can be a challenge in adolescence because your feelings come and go rapidly and it feels like you don't have any control over them. However, even though it might be a bit difficult, changing your thoughts can help you change your feelings.

Take this example. You are at the mall, standing in front of the door to the music store, and a woman pushes you aside roughly and rushes past you. How do you feel? Most people might initially feel irritated because they would think that the woman's behavior was rude and there was no reason for it. But suppose you had been inside the store and had heard the woman being paged to the parking lot because her son had been hit by a car. Now would you be irritated? Probably not. You changed your thoughts on the basis of new information, and consequently your feelings changed.

All too often we jump to conclusions and assume things, and in turn we experience certain feelings. If we assume bad or negative things, we feel more negatively. If we assume positive or good things, we feel more positively. Of course, the positive feelings aren't the ones that give us the trouble. It's the negative ones.

Agreeable to Argumentative

DISCUSSION–PAGE 2

Here's the process for changing your thoughts and feelings:

► First, you think about the situation, and when you do this,
  you probably have a feeling about it. Identify the situation and
  the feeling, as in the following example:

  > Your friend told you earlier in the week that she would invite
  > you to stay overnight, but yesterday she said it wouldn't work
  > out. You feel _____.

► Next, identify what you are thinking about this event. If you are mad or
  upset, you might be thinking: She doesn't like me anymore; she invited
  someone else; she doesn't want to be my friend anymore. On the other
  hand, if you were just disappointed instead of mad and upset, you might
  be thinking: Just because I can't stay overnight, it doesn't necessarily
  mean that we're not still friends or that she invited someone else. Maybe
  her mom or dad wouldn't let her have anyone over. It probably doesn't
  mean she doesn't like me.

Do you see the difference? When you were upset, you were assuming the worst,
and when you were less upset, you weren't reading things into the situation.
This is what you can do to get your feelings off the low end of the continuum
and move them up toward the high end.

See what you can do with the following example:

1. Marcus got a *D* on his world geography test. He was very upset
   with himself. What was he thinking?

2. If he wanted to be less upset, what could he think?

*Now make up your own example, and see if you can identify a way to
change thoughts in order to change feelings. Remember, you may not jump
all the way from the low end to the high end of the continuum, but by
changing how you think, you can move more toward the middle and
therefore feel better.*

Mood Management

Developmental Perspective

The ups and downs of adolescence occur because of the hormonal changes taking place in the body. Adolescents often feel powerless to control these mood swings, and they often become overwhelmed and discouraged when they can't manage their mood cycles. Being overwhelmed and discouraged can easily lead to unhealthy expression of feelings or impulsive actions that may have long-lasting negative consequences. Teaching adolescents to manage their moods is critical.

Objectives

▷ To identify effective strategies for managing moods

▷ To distinguish between helpful and unhelpful mood management strategies

Materials

▷ Paper, pencils, a sheet of newsprint, and a marker for every group of four students

▷ A roll of masking tape

▷ A Mood Management–Sorting Board (Handout 7) and an envelope of Mood Management–Game Cards (Handout 8) for each group of four students

Procedure

1. Introduce the activity by discussing the information in the Developmental Perspective. Divide students into groups of four and distribute a sheet of newsprint and a marker to each group. Have each group select a recorder to list their ideas on the newsprint. Ask students to discuss what they do to manage their moods. When they are finished, have the groups share ideas. Post the newsprint lists of suggestions for future reference.

2. Give each group a Mood Management–Sorting Board (Handout 7) and an envelope of Mood Management–Game Cards (Handout 8). Explain that group members should read the cards in the envelope and sort them into the spaces on the sorting board. Allow time for students to complete the activity, and then discuss the Content and Personalization Questions.

Discussion

CONTENT QUESTIONS

1. Was it hard for your group to identify things you do to help you manage your moods? Were your ideas similar to those proposed by the other groups?

2. Was it difficult to decide where to place the mood management suggestions on the sorting board? Which ones were the easiest? Which ones were the most difficult for you? Were you and your partners in agreement about which suggestions to put in each space?

3. Think about the items you put in the space for negative consequences. Why do you think people try these things to help themselves feel better? Do they really work long term?

PERSONALIZATION QUESTIONS

1. Have you tried any of these ideas to manage your moods? Which ones worked the best for you?

2. Which ideas seem like the most logical ones for you to try the next time you experience some moodiness?

3. Have you ever tried something to help yourself feel better in the short term but experienced negative consequences in the long run? (Invite sharing.)

4. What could you do to avoid trying things that might have negative long-term consequences even though you think they help you feel better in the short term?

5. What is one thing you will think about based on the information you learned in this activity?

Follow-up Activity

After several days, hold a follow-up discussion to see which ideas students are trying and what seems to be working best for them.

Mood Management

SORTING BOARD

Instructions: Read the cards in your envelope, and sort them into the five spaces on this sorting board.

Very Helpful
Somewhat Helpful
Not at All Helpful
Not Helpful/Negative Consequences
Could Be either Helpful or Unhelpful

Mood Management

GAME CARDS

Leader note: Copy and cut apart; give one envelope of cards to each group of four students.

Listen to loud music	Take prescribed medication, such as an antidepressant
Write poetry	Change your thinking so you don't make assumptions and upset yourself
Write letters to people you're upset with	
Do something physical like jog, shoot baskets, or take a walk	Attempt suicide
	Cut yourself up (self-mutilation)
Stop eating (starve yourself)	Take it out on other people
Binge eat (just keep on eating and eating)	
	Just leave the scene
Tell someone off	Get drunk or stoned
Punch something, like a pillow	
	Talk to a parent
Punch something, like a door or a wall	Talk to a teacher or a counselor
Distract yourself by watching television or reading	Talk to a friend

The Emotional Roller Coaster

Developmental Perspective

Although the emotional ups and downs that characterize early adolescence are generally less prevalent at this stage of development, the degree to which mid-adolescents experience mood swings depends on when they entered puberty. Therefore, it is not at all uncommon for 15- and 16-year-olds to experience these ups and downs.

Objective

▷ To develop an understanding of the up-and-down moods that characterize adolescence

Materials

▷ A copy of The Emotional Roller Coaster–Story (Handout 9), pencil, and paper for each student

Procedure

1. Introduce the activity by having students quickly brainstorm words that come to mind around the term *roller coaster*. Briefly discuss the fact that some people would liken adolescence to a roller coaster ride because of the emotional ups and downs that characterize this period of development.

2. Distribute a copy of The Emotional Roller Coaster–Story (Handout 9) to each student and ask students to read it.

3. When students have finished reading the story, ask them to respond to the questions at the end.

4. Discuss the Content and Personalization Questions.

Discussion

CONTENT QUESTIONS

1. What were some of the feelings the teenager in the story experienced?

2. What caused her to feel the way she did?

3. What did she try to do to manage her feelings more effectively?

PERSONALIZATION QUESTIONS

    1. Did you identify with the teenager in the story? If so, in what ways?

    2. If you have experienced ups and downs like these, what have you tried to do to help yourself deal with them?

Follow-up Activity

Invite students to write about their mood swings and how they try to cope with them. Give them the option of sharing their experiences in small groups.

The Emotional Roller Coaster

STORY—PAGE 1

Name: _____ Date: _____

Instructions: Read this true story, then answer the questions at the end.

I am 15. For the past several months I have been having lots of mood swings. I can wake up in the morning feeling excited about going to school to see my friends. But before I even get out the door I might be in a bad mood. Maybe it's something as little as not getting my hair to look right or not liking what I have to wear. But most of the time I just feel down for no apparent reason; there doesn't seem to be anything major that makes me feel the way I do. Oh, sometimes I may get in a fight with a friend, or I might get mad at my mom if she won't let me do something I want to do, but usually the moods just happen with no warning. Once I get to school I may snap out of it, but if I don't, I don't even want to talk to anybody.

The bad part of it is that when I feel down, I get scared. Sometimes it seems like the bad feelings will never go away, and I feel like giving up. When I'm down I tend to think of other things that make me feel more down, and then it just gets worse. It confuses me that I can feel that bad, and then those moods can shift and I can feel real up and happy. That's how I'd like to feel more of the time. Then I can laugh, do crazy things with my friends, and just feel good.

Sometimes when I'm down I get argumentative. I'll yell at my mom or go off on my friends for no good reason. Then later I feel guilty because I acted like that. The last time I was with my dad I blew up at him in the restaurant. People started looking at me and I felt pretty embarrassed. It's not like I really planned to act that way; I just didn't feel like I had any control. The one thing that helps get me out of the bad moods is to force myself to get out and do something. It takes a lot of effort, but if I do it, I usually feel better. I know that when I mope around I think about things that don't help my moods, so I try to stay "up" by getting involved in something other than myself. That isn't a guarantee that I'll stay "up," but at least it helps for a while. Doing things with my friends helps, too. We can have fun just hanging out.

The Emotional Roller Coaster

STORY–PAGE 2

I don't mean it to sound like I have a terrible life or am depressed all the time. It's not like that. I think I'm a pretty normal teenager. But sometimes no matter how hard I try it just isn't quite enough, and the moods take over. I know a lot of my friends feel like this, too. I guess we just have to ride the "roller coaster" and try not to let things get to us. I keep trying to remind myself that this won't last forever, and that helps.

–Liz, Age 16

1. Do you think this teenager's feelings are a normal part of adolescence?

2. Why do you think she gets scared when she feels the way she does?

3. Do you think it works to force yourself to do things even if you don't want to?

4. Have you experienced feelings similar to those expressed in this story? If so, how have you dealt with them?

Anger Is . . .

Developmental Perspective

Anger is a very prevalent emotion for adolescents, although many express it in inappropriate ways. Helping them understand how to deal effectively with anger facilitates a major part of their emotional development.

Objectives

▷ To learn more about anger and where it comes from

▷ To learn effective ways to deal with anger

Materials

▷ A chalkboard

▷ A copy of the Anger Is–Worksheet (Handout 10) for each student

▷ A copy of the Anger Is–Poem (Handout 11) for each student

▷ A pencil for each student

Procedure

1. Introduce the lesson by distributing the Anger Is–Worksheet (Handout 10) to each student. Ask students to read the handout and quickly decide whether they agree or disagree with each item. When they have finished, have them discuss their responses with a partner and then discuss items of agreement and disagreement with the total group.

2. Distribute the Anger Is–Poem (Handout 11) to each student. Ask each one to read the poem and write a brief reaction at the bottom of the page. Elicit discussion about the reactions.

3. Ask students to find new partners and brainstorm effective ways to deal with anger. Have pairs share their responses with the total group. Record responses on the board.

4. Explain that anger is a powerful emotion that sometimes gets out of control. Note that if people can reduce intense anger to irritation or mild anger, they are less likely to say things they don't mean or do things that could have negative consequences. Invite students to comment on this perspective:

   Anger comes from the expectation that things should be a certain way, and when the expectation is not fulfilled, the angry person thinks that the situation is horrible and that he or she can't stand it. By challenging these thoughts and recognizing that things don't always go the way he or she thinks they should (and that it is usually not the end of the world), a person can often reduce the intensity of the anger. It is also useful to ask whether anger helps. Do yelling, fighting, and name-calling usually help or hurt a relationship? There may be more effective ways of expressing anger if the intensity is reduced so the person is more in control.

5. Discuss the Content and Personalization Questions.

Discussion

CONTENT QUESTIONS

1. Do you think it is possible to avoid being angry? Why or why not?
2. Do you think anger has to control you? If not, how can you prevent it from controlling you?
3. Do you think it is helpful to get angry? Why or why not?

PERSONALIZATION QUESTIONS

1. Is anger an emotion you experience frequently?
2. What is the most effective thing you have ever done to deal with anger?
3. Have you ever tried reducing the intensity of your anger by changing the way you think? If so, how effective has this been for you?
4. What ideas did you learn from this lesson that you could apply the next time you feel angry?

Follow-up Activity

Invite students to write their own poems about anger.

Anger Is . . .

WORKSHEET

Name: _____ Date: _____

Instructions: Read the following statements. For each one, mark whether you agree (A) or disagree (D).

_____ 1. Anger is an emotion that can control your life.

_____ 2. Being angry can range from being a little ticked off to being in a violent rage.

_____ 3. When anger turns violent, you need help to control it.

_____ 4. You can control your anger.

_____ 5. Anger is common among teenagers.

_____ 6. Anger can make you feel powerful.

_____ 7. Feeling angry is better than feeling sad.

_____ 8. Anger can be caused by stress and tension.

_____ 9. It is better to let your anger out than to keep it in.

_____ 10. You can choose not to be angry.

Anger Is . . .

POEM

Anger is inside you.

It burns you, like the gates of hell.

It controls, fills you up.

Anger is red.

It is hot, like the sun.

It is powerful, like money.

Anger takes hold.

It grabs your arms and your legs.

It breaks you down.

Anger is a bright flash.

It is the emotional battle you're trying to win.

You against anger, who's keeping score?

–Mark, Age 17

Fights with Friends

Developmental Perspective

Peers continue to play an important role for adolescents at this stage. If they have attained formal operational thinking, their relationships will be more mature. However, for many adolescents, friendships can still be unstable, characterized by fights that usually result in hurt feelings. Because peers are such a significant part of teenagers' lives, they need skills for dealing with friendship issues.

Objectives

▷ To identify the reasons that friends argue

▷ To develop skills for dealing with friendship problems

Materials

▷ Paper and pencil for each student

▷ A roll of masking tape, a marker, and several sheets of newsprint for each group of four students

Procedure

1. Introduce the lesson by asking each student to take out paper and pencil and quickly list three words he or she would use to describe a friend. Briefly discuss the results with the total group. Then ask each student to list at least five things that friends argue and fight about.

2. Divide students into groups of four, and have each group appoint a recorder. Distribute newsprint, masking tape, and a marker to each group. Explain that each group's task is to take members' individual lists of the reasons friends argue and come to a group consensus on three reasons. Next, each group should discuss what they consider the best ways to deal with these friendship issues and have the recorder list up to six specific suggestions on the newsprint.

3. Ask each group to select a person to present the results to the rest of the group, and allow time for groups to present. Post the newsprint sheets with the responses in the room for future reference.

4. Discuss the Content and Personalization Questions.

Discussion

CONTENT QUESTIONS

1. Did your group easily reach consensus on the reasons friends argue and fight?
2. Did your group easily reach agreement on things to do to handle these friendship issues? Which ideas seem the most reasonable to you?
3. Do you think fighting between friends is a significant problem for your age group? Why or why not?

PERSONALIZATION QUESTIONS

1. Have you used any of the ideas that were presented today in dealing with your friendship fights? If so, how have they worked for you?
2. Do you and your friends argue very much? If so, is this something you would rather not experience? How do you think you could reduce the amount of time you spend arguing? (Invite students who don't argue with friends very often to share with others why this doesn't occur in their relationships.)

Follow-up Activity

Have each student select one of the ideas presented to implement. Provide time for students to report back on how this worked.

Rational Relationships

Developmental Perspective

Although some adolescents at this stage have developed abstract thinking skills, many still have not. Consequently, they still tend to conceptualize things in an either-or framework, overgeneralize and jump to conclusions about issues, and upset themselves by thinking irrationally when confronted with relationship issues.

Objectives

▷ To learn rational thinking skills

▷ To apply rational thinking skills to relationship problems

Materials

▷ Paper and pencil for each student

▷ A blank sheet of newsprint and a sheet of newsprint with the following written on it:

Assuming things without checking out the facts

Blowing the situation out of proportion; making more of it than it really is

Miscommunication

Closed-mindedness or defensiveness

Acting impulsively

Distorting reality

Procedure

1. Introduce the lesson by asking each student to think about a negative relationship involving a peer, a parent, or a teacher. Have students write brief descriptions of the problems without identifying the individuals. Explain that these writings will be for personal use only.

2. Post the sheet of newsprint, and indicate that the items listed are some of the factors that commonly result in relationship difficulties. Clarify any questions that students might have about the items and ask if they can think of others to add to the list. Ask each student to identify one or more of these (or other) factors that may have contributed to personal relationship difficulties. Discuss findings with the total group.

3. Read aloud the following example to illustrate the problems that can occur because of the factors listed on the newsprint. When you come to each parenthetical phrase, pause and ask students to identify which of the factors is being described.

> Christie is walking down the hall and sees Theresa talking to another girl. As Christie gets closer, Theresa and the other girl start to walk away and act like they don't want to talk to her. Christie assumes that they are talking about her and that Theresa is mad at her for some reason (assuming things without checking out the facts). Christie gets upset and decides that even though she had invited Theresa to her house after school to work on a project, she will go to the library instead and just not be home in case Theresa comes over (acting impulsively). When Christie is at the library, she writes a note to Theresa and tells her that she can't stand to be ignored and that she doesn't see how they can ever be friends again (blowing the situation out of proportion; making more of it than it really is). She sticks the note in Theresa's locker the next morning.

> Christie ignores Theresa all morning. At lunch, Theresa comes over and asks Christie why she wasn't home last night so they could work on their project. Christie angrily replies that she isn't about to work with someone who ignores her all the time (blowing the situation out of proportion; closed-mindedness; miscommunication). Theresa says she doesn't understand what Christie is talking about . . . but if she wants to act like that, it's her choice.

4. Discuss what happened in this situation and how the problem was easily distorted and blown out of proportion because of the assumptions that were made. Ask students whether such things happen in their interactions, and then discuss how to prevent these things from occurring. Write the following rational suggestions on the blank sheet of newsprint and use the information in parentheses to support the concept:

   ► Distinguish between a fact and an assumption. (In this case, the fact was that Christie saw her friend talking to another girl and starting to walk away; the assumption was that the friend was mad at her.)

   ► Don't make mountains out of molehills. (In this situation, Christie's friend was apparently ignoring her that day. That didn't mean that she would ignore her for the rest of her life.)

   ► Don't miscommunicate by reading too much into things or being defensive. (In this case, Christie read too much into the situation; she assumed that the friend's ignoring her meant that she didn't want to be friends with her.)

► Don't act impulsively on what you think are facts. (By impulsively deciding not to stay home, Christie might have made matters worse. Theresa might not have considered the situation to be a big problem until she got stood up by Christie or got a nasty note from her. Make sure you are clear about what the reality is before you act on perceptions. The reality in this case was that one friend ignored another; the idea that it was a major event that should ruin their friendship is a distortion.)

5. Discuss the Content and Personalization Questions.

Discussion

CONTENT QUESTIONS

1. Do you think that some or all of the factors listed here can cause problems in relationships?

2. How do you think Christie and Theresa's situation might have been different if they had followed the rational suggestions?

3. Do you think these problems are equally prevalent with boys and with girls? Why or why not?

PERSONALIZATION QUESTIONS

1. Have you or has someone you know had relationship problems because of some of the factors that were identified? (Invite sharing.)

2. What do you think would happen if you used the rational suggestions when problems occurred in your relationships with others?

Follow-up Activity

Have each student identify a recent relationship problem and analyze it according to the factors that contribute to relationship problems. Then encourage students to utilize the rational suggestions the next time they have problems and write short reports about whether the suggestions helped them in dealing with the problems.

Peers & Pressure

Developmental Perspective

Because adolescents at this stage are still striving for social acceptance, peers continue to play a very important role. Peer pressure is a factor in many relationships and is often the vehicle for inclusion and acceptance.

Objectives

▷ To examine the positive and negative aspects of peer pressure

▷ To identify the consequences of resisting peer pressure

Materials

▷ A chalkboard

▷ Paper and pencil for each student

▷ The following 12 words or phrases written (one per card) on 5 × 8–inch index cards:

    Drinking beer/alcohol

    Smoking cigarettes

    Engaging in sex

    Using pot/crank/cocaine

    Stealing

    Cheating

    Lying to parents

    Sneaking out of the house

    Getting good grades

    Staying sober

    Staying "clean"

    Performing in sports, music, drama

Procedure

1. Introduce the lesson by writing the phrase *peer pressure* on the board. Engage students in a discussion about what this term means, and elicit examples of both positive and negative peer pressure.

2. Divide students into groups of four and give each group one or two of the index cards with words or phrases. Have each group discuss how they think peers exert pressure on others to engage in the activity indicated on the card. Have each group appoint a recorder to write the ideas on the back of the card.

3. Allow time for the small groups to share their responses with the total group. Then engage students in a discussion about what they think they can do to resist peer pressure and what the consequences will be if they do.

4. Have students take out paper and pencils. Ask each one to identify a personal example of peer pressure (either positive or negative) and briefly describe it. In addition, students should indicate how they felt in the identified situations and how they handled the situations. (Stress that these responses will not be shared with others.) In conclusion, ask students to identify consequences of resisting or not resisting peer pressure in the situations they identified.

5. Discuss the Content and Personalization Questions.

Discussion

CONTENT QUESTIONS

1. Do you think peer pressure is good or bad? Is there such a thing as "good" peer pressure?

2. Do you think there is a lot of pressure from peers to do things like smoke, drink, or engage in sex?

3. What do you think is the most difficult thing about resisting peer pressure?

4. When you think about peer pressure, are you afraid that if you resist it you won't have friends? In reality, do you actually think this could happen, or is it just an assumption? Even if those peers never have anything to do with you, does that mean nobody would?

5. How does resisting peer pressure affect relationships with peers, positively or negatively?

PERSONALIZATION QUESTIONS

1. If you have experienced peer pressure, how did you feel about being pressured?

2. If you have experienced peer pressure and given in to it, did you think of the consequences before you gave in?

3. If you have experienced peer pressure, how did you feel about the way you handled it?

Follow-up Activity

Ask each student to write a "Dear Ann Landers" letter about a current problem with peer pressure and a response suggesting a way to handle the pressure.

Feedback from Friends

Developmental Perspective

Because friends play such an important role in adolescents' lives, the feedback they receive from others can have a major impact. Unfortunately, adolescents often lack the skills necessary to give and receive feedback appropriately.

Objectives

▷ To identify different styles of giving and receiving feedback

▷ To develop skills in giving and receiving feedback

Materials

▷ A copy of the Feedback from Friends–Questionnaire (Handout 12), the Feedback from Friends–Information Sheet (Handout 13), and the Feedback from Friends–Situations (Handout 14) for each student

▷ A pencil for each student

Procedure

1. Introduce the lesson by asking students to define the word *feedback* (a process by which people give and receive information about behavior or attitudes). Engage students in a brief discussion about how they feel when they get feedback and how they feel when they give it. Encourage them to identify various ways in which people give feedback, and ask them to consider whether the way it is received depends in part on the way it is delivered.

2. Distribute the Feedback from Friends–Questionnaire (Handout 12) to each student. Ask students to complete the questionnaire and share responses with a partner. Then distribute the Feedback from Friends–Information Sheet (Handout 13), about feedback styles, to each one. Ask students to read the information and fill in the blanks.

3. Distribute the Feedback from Friends–Situations (Handout 14) to each student. Then break students into triads. Assign each member of the triad a role: sender, receiver, or observer. Starting with Situation 1, ask the senders to give feedback to the receivers, practicing what they learned from the information sheet. Ask the observers to note how the feedback was delivered and received and report back to the senders and receivers. Rotate roles, and repeat the process, using Situations 2 and 3. After all three group members have assumed each role, discuss the experience of giving and receiving feedback, and compare students' comments to the information on the Feedback from Friends–Information Sheet.

4. Discuss the Content and Personalization Questions.

Discussion

CONTENT QUESTIONS

1. What did you learn about yourself by completing the questionnaire?
2. What did you learn about the three ways of receiving feedback?
   Do you agree with the points made in this handout?
3. What did you learn about the ways to give feedback?

PERSONALIZATION QUESTIONS

1. What is your style for receiving feedback? How does this style work for you?
2. What is your style for giving feedback? How do you feel about this style?
3. On the basis of what you learned from this lesson, is there anything you would like to change about the way you give and/or receive feedback? (Invite sharing.)

Follow-up Activity

Have students work in small groups to generate additional situations similar to the Feedback from Friends–Situations (Handout 14). Collect the situations from each group and then ask students to form new groups, each with a sender, a receiver, and an observer. Distribute the situations, and have students practice giving and receiving feedback.

Feedback from Friends

QUESTIONNAIRE

Name: _____ Date: _____

Instructions: Read each item, and check the response that best describes you. Discuss your responses with a partner.

1. When a friend gives me feedback, I take it seriously and try to do something about the situation if it is something the friend thinks I need to change.

   Like me ☐   Sometimes like me ☐   Not like me ☐

2. When I give feedback to a friend, I try to imagine how he or she would feel and deliver the message in a sensitive manner.

   Like me ☐   Sometimes like me ☐   Not like me ☐

3. When someone gives me negative feedback, I immediately assume that I am to blame or that there is something wrong with me.

   Like me ☐   Sometimes like me ☐   Not like me ☐

4. When I give feedback, I say exactly what I mean and don't think about how the other person will take it.

   Like me ☐   Sometimes like me ☐   Not like me ☐

5. When I receive negative feedback, I usually feel upset.

   Like me ☐   Sometimes like me ☐   Not like me ☐

6. I usually don't give feedback to friends because I am afraid they won't like me if I say it.

   Like me ☐   Sometimes like me ☐   Not like me ☐

7. When I receive feedback, I usually get defensive.

   Like me ☐   Sometimes like me ☐   Not like me ☐

8. When I receive positive feedback, I usually discount it.

   Like me ☐   Sometimes like me ☐   Not like me ☐

Feedback from Friends

INFORMATION SHEET–PAGE 1

Name: _____ Date: _____

Instructions: Read the information, which describes different feedback styles. When you come to the questions, write your answers in the blanks.

There are three main ways in which people receive feedback:

► They immediately internalize what the other person has said and assume that everything said is true.

► They immediately discount what the other person is saying and reject the feedback.

► They think about what has been said, reject the parts they don't think are true, and accept what they think might have some merit.

There is a danger in the first style. Suppose you receive feedback from someone indicating that you are insensitive. If you immediately assume that what the person said is true and you get upset about it, you engage in self-downing, which means that you put yourself down. You don't stop to consider that this is only one person's perception. Although it may be true (at least with that person, at least some of the time), you easily assume that everyone thinks this way about you, and you get very down on yourself.

There is also a danger in the second style. Go back to the previous example. When you receive feedback from one person indicating that you are insensitive, you immediately discount it. You assume that it's that person's opinion and think that he or she doesn't know anything. Now, here's the danger: It may be true that you are insensitive to this person, so the feedback would be valid (at least as it applies to this person, at least some of the time). If you discount the feedback, your behavior won't change.

The third style is obviously the preferred one. You receive some feedback, and you think about it objectively. You ask yourself, "Is what the person said about me true?" It may be, in which case you can choose to change your behavior if you don't like hearing this feedback. Or, if this person's opinion doesn't matter to you, you may choose to discount it. Here's the advantage of this style: Although you may acknowledge that this person's feedback is accurate, you don't put yourself down, assuming that everyone thinks this way about you and that you are always insensitive and therefore a no-good person.

Feedback from Friends

INFORMATION SHEET–PAGE 2

We have been focusing on negative feedback. But sometimes people even discount positive feedback, assuming that it is just one person's opinion and that the person doesn't really know much. This is why it is much better to adopt the third style: Carefully examine what you think is accurate, but do so without putting yourself down or discounting the feedback as invalid, at least until you have reflected on it.

Which is your style for receiving feedback? _____

_____

The way you deliver feedback is also important to consider. Are you so blunt and to the point that the other person gets defensive or upset by what you say? What you say may be very valid, but the way you say it has a lot to do with the way the other person receives it. For example, suppose you want to tell a friend that you think he is overreacting to an issue with his girlfriend. You could deliver a "you" message, such as this: "You're so defensive about this stuff with your girlfriend. You're always overreacting to her. Just cool it." Or you could deliver an "I" message, such as this: "I think you sometimes overreact to what your girlfriend is doing, and maybe if you didn't, the two of you would get along better."

Do you see a difference in styles? Which style do you think would be the most effective? Does it depend at all on the type of friendship you have with a person? There is a third option: You could just keep quiet and not say anything. But the danger in keeping quiet is that sometimes, depending on the issue, your feelings about the other person become more and more negative to the point that you don't want to associate with him or her, and then you may jeopardize the relationship.

Which is your style for giving feedback? _____

_____

Feedback from Friends

SITUATIONS

Instructions: Use these situations to practice giving and receiving feedback. Your leader will give you detailed directions.

Situation 1

For several weeks your friend has been very abrupt and rude—not just to you, but to lots of other students, too. You think it is affecting his (or her) relationships, and you decide to say something.

        Sender: Deliver the message.

      Receiver: React/respond to the message.

      Observer: Note how the sender delivered the message and how this affected the way it was received. Also note how the receiver responded.

Situation 2

You hear several students talking about how one of your friends is starting to hang out with a bad group of kids. You personally don't associate with this group, and you are worried about your friend. You decide to say something to her (or him).

        Sender: Deliver the message.

      Receiver: React/respond to the message.

      Observer: Note how the sender delivered the message and how this affected the way it was received. Also note how the receiver responded.

Situation 3

You can hardly stand to be around your locker mate because he (or she) is always running people down and is negative about everything. You decide to say something to him (or her).

        Sender: Deliver the message.

      Receiver: React/respond to the message.

      Observer: Note how the sender delivered the message and how this affected the way it was received. Also note how the receiver responded.

Think, Feel, Do

Developmental Perspective

Depending on the rate of maturation, 15-year-olds may begin thinking more abstractly, a development that enables them to put problems in better perspective and think more seriously about consequences. If they understand the connections between their thoughts, feelings, and actions, they can become more adept at addressing situational and developmental stressors.

Objective

▷ To learn how thoughts influence feelings and actions

Materials

▷ A chalkboard

▷ A copy of the Think, Feel, Do–Worksheet (Handout 15) and a pencil for each student

Procedure

1. Read the following short scenario to students and ask several to describe how they would feel in this situation:

   You studied a long time last night for an exam. This is not one of your easiest subjects. Today is the day of the exam. The teacher walks in and says the test is postponed until tomorrow.

2. After you have elicited several feelings (which presumably will be different), ask students why some of them would feel relieved, some disappointed, and so on. Show them that what they think about the event influences the feeling: If they feel they still need more study time since this is a hard subject and they want to do well, they may feel relieved. If they just want to get the test over with, they may feel disappointed. If they don't care, this indifference will also affect their feelings. Stress the connection between thoughts and feelings and ask students to share other examples. Explain that when people have strong negative feelings, they are usually thinking that something is really awful; that they can't stand it; that what happened isn't fair or shouldn't have occurred; or that something must be wrong with them, that they are bad or to blame. Apply this explanation to the earlier scenario: If some students thought it was awful that the test got postponed because they couldn't stand the anxiety for another day, they would be more upset than if they just saw the postponement as an inconvenience.

3. Introduce the concept that the way a person feels influences the way a person acts. Ask each student to think about a recent occasion when he or she felt angry. Elicit from students how they acted when they were angry, and list the various behaviors on the board. (For example, some may have lashed out at others, some may have kept the anger inside, and others may have punched someone or something.)

4. Distribute the Think, Feel, Do–Worksheet (Handout 15) to each student. Ask each one to complete the worksheet and then discuss responses with two other students.

5. After some discussion time, show students that they can change the way they feel and act by changing the way they think. Refer to the first situation on the worksheet. Explain that if the student was upset about not making first chair, he or she might be thinking that the situation was unfair, in which case the student would probably feel angry and might lash out at the teacher. Or the student might feel worthless, grow depressed, and avoid others for a while. To change the depressed feelings and the behaviors, the student would have to ask him- or herself: "Am I really totally worthless because I didn't make first chair? Just because I didn't make it, does that mean I don't have any talent?" After asking a series of challenging questions, the student should have a better perspective on the situation. Although the upset feelings might persist, the student would feel less self-deprecating and be less depressed. If the student thought the teacher was unfair, the challenging questions would have to be different. "Can I control what the teacher does? Even if I don't think it is fair, he must have his reasons. I guess everything isn't always fair. Does it really do me any good to get so upset about it?" Once again, even though the upset feelings would remain, the student would be less angry after challenging his or her thoughts. In a less angry, more calm state, the student could perhaps discuss the situation with the teacher, using an assertive rather than aggressive communication style.

6. Ask students to work in their groups to identify challenging questions for the second and their own situations and to predict how raising those questions would change feelings and behaviors.

7. Discuss the Content and Personalization Questions.

Discussion

Content Questions

1. Did you have any difficulty identifying thoughts, feelings, and actions for the examples on the worksheet?

2. What is the connection between what you think, feel, and do?

3. When you and others in your group worked on the challenging questions, what did you learn by doing this? Can you see how asking these questions can affect how you feel and how you act?

PERSONALIZATION QUESTIONS

1. Look back at the personal situations you identified on the worksheet. How hard was it to identify your thoughts, feelings, and actions?

2. Have you been in a situation where you changed your thoughts and, as a result, your feelings and behaviors changed? (Invite sharing of examples.)

3. How do you think you can apply what you have learned about thoughts, feelings, and behaviors to problems you are experiencing in your life?

Follow-up Activity

Ask each student to identify thoughts, feelings, and behaviors regarding at least one situation in the coming week. Then have students go back and ask themselves challenging questions to help change the thoughts, feelings, and behaviors. Give students time to report back on how this process worked for them.

Think, Feel, Do

WORKSHEET

Name: _____ Date: _____

Instructions: Read the first two situations and identify possible feelings and behaviors. Then think of a situation from your own life, and do the same for it.

Situation 1

You play in the high school orchestra and have been trying to make first-chair violin. After your last lesson, the teacher told you that you aren't good enough to make first chair. Orchestra is really important to you.

1. What would you be thinking?

2. How would you feel?

3. How would you act? What would you do with your feeling?

Situation 2

You tried out for the lead role in the school play and didn't make it. The day after you learned that you didn't get the role, you heard two friends in the locker room talking about you. They were saying that it served you right not to get the lead since you seemed so sure you would get it.

1. What would you be thinking?

2. How would you feel?

3. How would you act? What would you do with your feeling?

Your Own Situation

_____

_____

_____

1. What would you be thinking?

2. How would you feel?

3. How would you act? What would you do with your feeling?

Awesome Outcome

Developmental Perspective

Although adolescents are often able to identify likely consequences of their decisions, many ignore the consequences because they don't care or they want to see what they can get away with. Unfortunately, some of their decisions can have long-lasting negative consequences. Helping them project ahead and think seriously about outcomes is critical.

Objectives

▷ To evaluate decisions and identify consequences

▷ To learn ways to change negative behaviors

Materials

▷ A copy of the Awesome Outcome–Story (Handout 16) and a pencil for each student

Procedure

1. Introduce the lesson by asking students to think about very good decisions they or other people they know have made. Then ask them to think about very bad decisions they or other people they know have made. Elicit discussion about good and bad types of decisions. Try to identify what makes a decision good or bad, stressing the relevance of long- and short-term consequences.

2. Distribute the Awesome Outcome–Story (Handout 16) to each student. Ask students to read the story and underline each decision. When they have finished, have each one list at least eight consequences of the decisions on the back of the handout.

3. Divide students into groups of four, and have them share the decisions they identified and the consequences they listed. Have them also discuss what they think caused the teenager in the story to turn around and stop making decisions that had negative consequences.

4. Discuss the Content and Personalization Questions.

Discussion

CONTENT QUESTIONS

1. What were some of the decisions the teenager in the story made?

2. Do you think he thought about consequences before he decided to do what he did?

3. What do you think finally made him think about the choices he was making?

PERSONALIZATION QUESTIONS

1. Do you take chances just to see what you can get by with, as the teenager in this story did? If so, have there been consequences for you?

2. Have you made decisions that you later regretted? If so, will this fact influence your behavior in the future?

3. Did you learn anything from this story that might have some application to your life?

Follow-up Activity

Have students write their own stories about awesome outcomes based on their own lives or the lives of their peers.

Awesome Outcome

STORY—PAGE 1

Name: _____ Date: _____

Instructions: Read the story, and underline each decision.

I was 14 years old and miserable. I wished I could just die. I had tried to end my life by taking a lot of pills, but all I did was make myself really sick. Then I started to cut my wrists and watch myself bleed, but that wasn't good enough, so I decided to do something that would make it quick and to the point. I went to my father's room, got one of his rifles, and loaded it. But once I got it loaded, I told two of my friends, and they talked me out of it. Right now I'm actually glad they did, but at the time I thought that they were just stopping me this time, but that I would eventually do it.

But because I still felt so bad, I started doing drugs as a way to take my pain away. Then I started skipping school. The administrator caught up with me and gave me truant notices and warned me not to let it happen again. Well, I did let it happen again and again, and it just wasn't enough. I wanted to see how far I could get if I just kept playing with the school system. It finally caught up with me, and I had in-school suspension until the end of the year.

Then the summer from hell came. I put my parents through a lot. I wouldn't come home until 2:00 or 3:00 in the morning. My mom was worried sick. She thought I was lying in a ditch dead because she never knew where I was or who I was with because I refused to tell her. I know she cried herself to sleep, but I didn't care much about that at the time. I was usually drunk or high. I experimented with a lot of drugs and thought drugs made me look like the coolest person. When I was high I thought everyone wanted to know me and hang out with me, but they didn't. Actually, a lot of people liked me better when I wasn't into drugs. But then I didn't care what they thought. The school year started, and I decided not to skip classes. I thought I'd be fine. But the first day, I skipped my fifth-hour class since it was right after lunch and I didn't feel like going back to school. Freshmen weren't even supposed to leave the building for lunch, but I did. I figured I wouldn't get caught. Then I started skipping more classes just to get high and take as many other drugs as I could so I could get through the rest of the day. I'd even go to class high as a kite and just sit there and try to listen.

Awesome Outcome

STORY–PAGE 2

After a couple of months, the administration caught on and came after me. They gave me three chances to shape up. My dad even came to school and followed me around to make sure I went to class. That was embarrassing. I decided to get my act together, and I didn't skip for about two weeks, but then it started again. This time I got kicked out and sent to a school discipline center. I hated it there. You could get detention for the littlest thing. I was a good student and I could look pretty innocent, so a lot of the teachers wondered why I was even there. But I eventually changed their minds because I got caught with cigarettes and eventually got suspended for a day because I always brought them to school. After that, I never brought cigarettes to school again.

I finally decided that I should buckle down and get all my work in and not get in trouble. If I did that, the principal said they would let me go back to my old school. I missed my friends and being in band. So I worked really hard, and after three months I got to go back. It was great to see all the friends that I hadn't seen for a long time. Now I have been back for about nine weeks and I haven't skipped once. I don't plan to, either. I don't want to end up back at the discipline center, and I don't think my life was going anywhere.

I look back on the choices I made over the last couple of years, and I think about how stupid I was. Every choice I made seems pointless now. I have quit skipping school, and although I still do get high occasionally, I don't do it nearly as much as I did. I got through all of this because my friends and family never doubted me and were always there for me through thick and thin. I would love to thank them for that, and now I know I can really count on them.

–Chris, Age 15

Problem-Solving Skills

Developmental Perspective

Adolescents often make problems worse for themselves because they make assumptions about how people will react, don't weigh the risks, or don't care what happens to them. All of these factors influence their problem-solving behavior. Helping young people develop problem-solving skills is essential at this stage of development.

Objective

▷ To learn effective problem-solving skills

Materials

▷ A chalkboard

▷ Paper and pencil for each student

▷ A sheet of newsprint with the following written on it:

> **Ineffective Problem-Solving Skills**
>
> Failing to check out assumptions
>
> Ignoring the risks
>
> Deciding to do something to "get back" at someone else
>
> Wanting to see how much you can get by with
>
> Not caring what happens to you

Procedure

1. Introduce the lesson by asking students to form groups of three and quickly brainstorm a list of effective problem-solving skills.

2. Allow time for each group to share its suggestions. Write the suggestions on the board under the heading "Effective Problem-Solving Skills." Then read the following:

   > Andrew was almost failing a class. He didn't think it would do any good to talk to the teacher. He assumed his parents would be really upset, so rather than say anything about it, he just stopped going to class. Finally, the school called his parents to let them know that he was skipping. When they talked to Andrew, they asked him why he'd never said anything to the teacher or to them about the trouble he was having, and he said he just assumed it wouldn't do any good.

Ask students what was faulty about Andrew's problem-solving process and what might have happened if he had done things differently. Discuss the concept of checking out assumptions as an important part of the problem-solving process.

3. Post the newsprint list of ineffective problem-solving skills, and ask each group to come up with an example of each of these (without using names).

4. Ask students to share their examples and discuss the problems that can occur when they attempt to make decisions or solve problems without checking out assumptions and weighing the risks; when they do something just to get back at someone or to see what they can get away with; or when they do something without caring what happens.

5. Discuss the Content and Personalization Questions.

Discussion

CONTENT QUESTIONS

1. Before this lesson, were you aware of the ineffective problem-solving skills? What makes them ineffective?

2. In the examples you identified, what might have happened if the people had used more effective skills?

3. Are there other examples of ineffective problem-solving skills? Other examples of effective problem-solving skills?

PERSONALIZATION QUESTIONS

1. When you've tried to solve a problem, have you ever used one of the ineffective problem-solving skills identified in this lesson? If so, how did this affect your ability to solve the problem?

2. How satisfied are you with your problem-solving skills? If there is something you would like to change, how will you do it?

3. Did you learn anything from this lesson that will help you solve problems more effectively in the future?

Follow-up Activity

Encourage students to reflect on their own problem-solving processes and identify things they consider especially effective or ineffective about their processes. Ask them to write about problem-solving strengths or areas that need to be improved (and how they will bring about the improvement). Ask them to comment especially on how their problem-solving skills affect their lives.

Realistic Reasoning

Developmental Perspective

Although by this stage of development many adolescents are more frequently utilizing abstract thinking skills, they often are not realistic in their assessment of situations. This lack of realism affects their responses to situations. Young people need to learn to correct thinking errors that often lead to self-defeating behaviors.

Objectives

▷ To develop skills in assessing situations realistically

▷ To develop skills in applying good reasoning

Materials

▷ A copy of the Realistic Reasoning–Vignettes (Handout 17) and a pencil for each student

Procedure

1. Introduce the activity by reading the following statements and asking students to raise their hands if a statement has ever applied to them:

   ► You think you absolutely can't stand something, but actually you can.

   ► You assume the blame for everything, even though it's not all your fault.

   ► You think other people should act the way you think they should.

   ► You think that everything in life should be fair.

   ► You think that you shouldn't have to experience any discomfort in your life.

2. Discuss the fact that the preceding are cognitive or thinking errors that influence the way people behave. Distribute the Realistic Reasoning–Vignettes (Handout 17) to each student, and ask students to read them. Have them underline the faulty reasoning in each vignette as they read.

3. After students have finished reading and underlining, have them discuss the faulty reasoning with a partner.

4. Discuss the Content and Personalization Questions.

Discussion

CONTENT QUESTIONS

1. Were you able to identify the faulty reasoning patterns in the vignettes? What do you think makes them faulty?

2. How do you think faulty reasoning affects behavior?

3. How common do you think these faulty reasoning patterns are?

PERSONALIZATION QUESTIONS

1. Have you (or have others you know) exercised faulty reasoning in the past? If so, how has this affected your (or their) behavior?

2. If you still have a tendency to use faulty reasoning, how do you think you can change your thinking so it is more realistic? (Elicit ideas and discuss the concepts of blowing things out of proportion, assuming things will never change, thinking one shouldn't have to work too hard at anything, "awfulizing" or thinking the worst, and thinking in the present without looking to the future.)

Follow-up Activity

Have students watch movies or television programs and look for examples of faulty reasoning. Ask students to put their examples in writing. Allow time to discuss them with the total group, reflecting on how outcomes would have been affected if clearer reasoning had been used.

Realistic Reasoning

VIGNETTES

Name: _____ Date: _____

Instructions: Read each vignette, and underline the faulty reasoning in each one.

1. Rob and Paula, age 15, had been going together for six months. It was a very serious relationship. One day Paula told Rob that she didn't want to be tied down and suggested they stop dating and just be friends. Rob couldn't stand the thought of losing Paula, and he knew he would never find someone he loved as much as he loved her. He went home, found his dad's gun, and shot himself because he knew he couldn't stand the pain of living without Paula.

2. NaTasha's parents were getting divorced. She and her mother were going to have to move away. NaTasha didn't think she could stand to be away from her friends, and she didn't want to have to finish her freshman year in a school where she wouldn't know anybody and would be miserable. She figured she'd never make friends there and it would be awful. She decided to run away.

3. Amy got into a big fight with her mother because her mother refused to let her stay out past 10:00 on school nights. Amy thought that was unreasonable, so she just went over to a friend's house and got high so she would forget about the argument.

4. Kim wanted to try out for cheerleading, but she thought she was too fat. She started exercising to get in shape, but that took too much time, and she hated to work out. She thought it would be easier to lose weight if she just stopped eating, but it was too hard to give up chips and candy. She finally started forcing herself to throw up so she could lose weight faster and not have to work so hard at it.

5. Pablo was failing social studies at midterm, so he stopped doing all his assignments because he figured he'd flunk the course regardless of what he did the rest of the term.

6. Gina's boyfriend was making good money dealing drugs. He dropped out of school. Gina thought that was a really dumb decision, but she still kept dating him, even though her friends said her reputation would be ruined if she continued to hang out with a dropout drug dealer. Gina ignored them; she didn't worry too much about how her reputation might be affected.

7. Carl wasn't selected to be in the honor band, so he quit. He figured he was a lousy player and had no future in music.

the **PASSPORT** PROGRAM

GRADE
10

Self-Development
ACTIVITY
1   Mirror, Mirror on the Wall
2   I Am Someone Who . . .
3   I Hate My Weight
4   Living Up to an Image

Emotional Development
ACTIVITY
1   Changing Feelings
2   Controlling Confusion
3   Peeling Away the Layers
4   Will I Ever Feel Better?

Social Development
ACTIVITY
1   Rumors and Relationships
2   Heartbreak and a Half
3   Growing Apart
4   Why Do They Treat Me like This?

Cognitive Development
ACTIVITY
1   Gain with Goals
2   Make a Decision
3   Weigh the Risks
4   Dangerous Decisions

Mirror, Mirror on the Wall

Developmental Perspective

Although by this stage of development adolescents are generally gaining self-confidence and beginning to establish themselves as individuals within a group, they do express their individuality–through clothing or hairstyles, for example. As they look in the mirror they no longer see children, but question who they will be as adults. And although they can think more abstractly, they still tend to see themselves as either all positive or all negative, not as persons with positive and negative traits.

Objective

▷ To distinguish between all-or-nothing self-rating and rating one's individual traits

Materials

▷ A mirror (several may be needed if the group is large)

▷ Paper and pencil for each student

Procedure

1. Introduce the lesson by passing the mirror around and asking students to look briefly at themselves. (If it seems too threatening for students to do this in a large group, hold up the mirror and ask them to imagine they are looking at themselves.)

2. Ask each student to take out paper and pencil and quickly write four positive things he or she saw when looking in the mirror.

3. Ask students to think about all aspects of themselves, not just appearance. Once again, ask each one to identify four positive assets (good skater, good listener, good leader, and the like).

4. Pass the mirror again (or have students imagine this), but this time have them identify up to four things they didn't like when they looked in the mirror. Then have each one list deficits unrelated to appearance (not good in sports, does poorly in math, and the like).

5. When students have finished writing, ask each one to turn the paper over, draw a big circle, and mark several pluses (+) and minuses (−) inside the circle.

6. Ask students to write some of the traits they previously identified next to the pluses and minuses in their circles.

7. Discuss the fact that people tend to rate themselves in an all-or-nothing way, when in reality everyone is a human being with lots of pluses and minuses. People can work to improve some of their minuses, but even if they never did so, they would still be good people. Emphasize the importance of not rating oneself as good or bad based on a single trait.

8. Discuss the Content and Personalization Questions.

Discussion

CONTENT QUESTIONS

1. Which were harder to identify, the positive or the negative traits?

2. What does it say about you if you have negative traits?

3. Do you think it is possible for anyone to have all positive traits? All negative traits?

PERSONALIZATION QUESTIONS

1. Which positive trait are you the most proud of?

2. Which negative trait would you most like to change? Do you think it is possible to do this, and if so, how?

3. Can you think of a time when you rated yourself as a good or a bad person on the basis of one aspect of yourself? For example, have you ever thought of yourself as a bad person if you performed horribly in a basketball game or on an exam? Are you, in fact, a bad person? (Invite sharing.)

4. What were the negative implications for you when you rated yourself negatively on the basis of one or a few negative qualities?

5. What message do you need to give yourself about who you are—a person with positive and negative traits?

Follow-up Activity

Have students write "I Accept Myself as a Person Who . . ." stories, incorporating the traits they identified in the activity as well as other aspects of themselves.

I Am Someone Who...

Developmental Perspective

Identity development is a major task during this phase of development. It is not uncommon for adolescents to change interests, plans, and friends or to adopt different mannerisms or beliefs in this identity search. All of this experimentation is an important part of young people's development.

Objective

▷ To clarify aspects of self-identity

Materials

▷ A copy of the I Am Someone Who–Sorting Board (Handout 1) and an envelope of I Am Someone Who–Sentence Slips (Handout 2) for each student

Procedure

1. Introduce the lesson by eliciting responses in gestures: Ask students to raise their hands and wave them in the air if they really think they know "who they are," to put their hands down and wave them around if they are unclear about who they are, and to put their palms out if they have some idea of who they are.

2. Distribute the I Am Someone Who–Sorting Board (Handout 1) and Sentence Slips (Handout 2) to each student. Ask students to read the sentence slips and sort them according to the categories on the sorting board.

3. When students have finished sorting, invite them to share their results with a partner.

4. Discuss the Content and Personalization Questions.

Discussion

CONTENT QUESTIONS

1. How easy was it for you to do the sorting?
2. Did you and your partner have similar sentence slips in the various categories?
3. Were any items particularly difficult to categorize? If so, which ones?

PERSONALIZATION QUESTIONS

1. On the basis of this activity, do you know yourself as well as you thought you did?
2. What, if anything, would you like to have in the "Very Much Like Me" category that isn't there now? How about the "Not at All Like Me" category?

3. On the basis of your responses to the previous question, are there things you would like to change about yourself? Is this possible? How can you do it? (Invite students to share specific examples.)

4. Suppose you can't change anything. Can you accept yourself as you are?

5. What did you learn about yourself from this activity?

Follow-up Activity

Ask students to set achievable goals to change items in the "Not at All Like Me" category that they would prefer to have in one of the "Like Me" categories.

I Am Someone Who

SORTING BOARD

Name: _____ Date: _____

Instructions: Read the sentence slips. Then place each one in the space on the sorting board that best tells how well the sentence describes you.

Very Much Like Me
Like Me
Somewhat Like Me
Not Very Much Like Me
Not at All Like Me

I Am Someone Who

SENTENCE SLIPS

Leader note: Copy and cut apart; give one set to each student.

I am someone who is dependable.	I am someone who is a hard worker.
I am someone who is a risk taker.	I am someone who is carefree.
I am someone who is responsible.	I am someone who gives in to peer pressure.
I am someone who is sensitive to others' feelings.	I am someone who thinks I have to be perfect.
I am someone who is a leader.	I am someone who is insecure.
I am someone who is a follower.	I am someone who puts on a "mask"; not many people really know who I am.
I am someone who is a "prep."	I am someone who is more sensitive than I let on.
I am someone who is honest with parents.	I am someone who gets angry easily.
I am someone who is concerned about doing well in school.	I am someone who feels inadequate in social situations.
I am someone who worries about what others think of me.	I am someone who manages my time well.
I am someone who worries about my future.	I am someone who is ashamed of some things I have done in the past.
I am someone who makes friends easily.	I am someone whom others look up to.
I am someone who adjusts well to new situations.	I am someone who feels happy about my life.
I am someone who stands up for my rights.	I am someone who can make mistakes and not get down on myself.
I am someone who is concerned about my reputation.	I am someone who is independent.

I Hate My Weight

Developmental Perspective

Stereotypes of the perfect body image exert a great deal of pressure on adolescents. In their quest to conform to ideal standards of beauty, increasing numbers of adolescent females are at risk for developing eating disorders. Eating disorders are becoming more common for young males, particularly for wrestlers who need to "make weight." These eating disorders are very serious, but because adolescents don't usually think about long-term consequences, they may fall victim before they realize what is happening.

Objectives

▷ To learn facts about anorexia and bulimia

▷ To identify the social, emotional, cognitive, and physical problems associated with eating disorders

Materials

▷ A chalkboard

▷ A copy of the I Hate My Weight–Fact Sheet (Handout 3) and the I Hate My Weight–Story (Handout 4) for each student

▷ A pencil for each student

Procedure

1. Introduce the lesson by writing the terms *anorexia* and *bulimia* on the board. Ask students to define these terms, listing as many characteristics as possible.

2. Distribute the I Hate My Weight–Fact Sheet (Handout 3) to each student, and ask students to read it. When they have finished, have each student list three things he or she learned about each disorder at the bottom of the worksheet. Ask students to discuss their responses with a partner.

3. Distribute the I Hate My Weight–Story (Handout 4) to each student. After students have had time to read it, have them identify in writing four effects of this teenager's battle with anorexia that made an impression on them. Ask students to share their impressions with partners.

4. Discuss the Content and Personalization Questions.

Discussion

CONTENT QUESTIONS

1. What did you learn about anorexia?
2. What did you learn about bulimia?
3. What are some of the short-term consequences of eating disorders?
4. What are some of the long-term consequences of eating disorders?
5. What was your impression of the struggle the teenager in this story waged against her eating disorder? What have been the long-term consequences for her?

PERSONALIZATION QUESTIONS

1. Have you or has anyone you know had problems with an eating disorder? If so, what have been the effects of this for you or for the person you know?
2. What did you learn from this lesson that might be helpful to you or others you know?

Follow-up Activity

Invite an eating disorders specialist or a nurse to talk about signs and symptoms. If possible, ask someone who is recovering from an eating disorder to discuss his or her experience.

I Hate My Weight

FACT SHEET–PAGE 1

Anorexia and bulimia are the two most serious eating disorders. With anorexia, people starve themselves because they have an intense fear of getting fat. They have very distorted body images and think they are still fat even after they have become seriously underweight. Anorexics become obsessed with food; they worry about what they can eat and how much. This obsession interferes with social life and school activities because the anorexic may not want to eat in public for fear of being noticed or teased. Anorexia is very serious and life threatening. If you do not eat enough, the major organs in your body stop functioning.

Bulimia is different from anorexia in that a bulimic eats large amounts of food at one time. This is often called binging. After eating, bulimics make themselves vomit. They may also use laxatives. An example of binging may be eating a large bag of chips followed by several sandwiches, a package of cookies, and two shakes. Because bulimics don't want to get fat, they get rid of their food by purging–inducing vomiting. Bulimic behavior shouldn't be confused with being hungry and eating a lot. If you are just a big eater, you won't binge and purge, and you won't be secretive about what and where you eat.

Bulimia is often practiced by wrestlers who are trying to "make weight." Bulimics are impulsive eaters and may steal money to buy food. Bulimia is also very serious, but it is easier to detect because of the binge/purge behavior.

I Hate My Weight

FACT SHEET—PAGE 2

Signs and Symptoms of Anorexia

Extreme weight loss

Extreme dissatisfaction with and distortion of body image

Excessive exercise

Intense worry about food—when, what, and how much to eat

Serious food restriction—having lists of "safe foods," which usually don't include any sweets or fat

Discontinuation of menstrual cycle in females; possible inability ever to have children

Guilt if the person eats too much or doesn't exercise

Withdrawal from social and school functions

Mood swings: depression, defiance, irritability, guilt, anger

Low self-esteem

Lack of energy

Signs and Symptoms of Bulimia

Rapid weight gain and weight loss

Being secretive about binging and purging

Developing scars on the fingers that have been used to start vomiting

Tooth decay and loss of enamel or gum disease

Extreme dissatisfaction with and distortion of body image

Frequent trips to the bathroom to vomit or abuse laxatives

Low self-esteem

Feelings of irritability, anger, guilt, depression, loneliness

I Hate My Weight

STORY—PAGE 1

I was 9 years old and hated my body. I remember thinking that if I were skinny, everything would be perfect and I'd be happy for the rest of my life. Little did I know what I was getting myself into.

All through elementary school I struggled with the way I looked. I was on a new diet every week. At the end of sixth grade I was tired of dieting, and I decided to go on one last diet—for good.

I started by not allowing myself to take second helpings at dinner. Then I stopped having snacks after school. I got out of eating breakfast by lying and saying that my stomach hurt or that I didn't feel well. I threw my lunch away at school so my mother wouldn't know I hadn't eaten. I didn't allow myself to eat any desserts, sweets, or anything with even a little bit of fat. I completely took meat out of my diet.

It wasn't hard to tell I had lost weight. I have a twin sister, and we had always looked exactly alike. Now, not only was I thinner, but I was much shorter. I was missing my growth spurt, but I didn't care at the time. My hair was falling out in clumps, but I didn't relate that to my lack of nutrition. I barely had energy to laugh, talk, or even smile. I would wear four layers of clothes and still feel like I was freezing to death. I became mean, selfish, and irritable.

However, I was very good at lying and keeping my life a huge secret from everyone. I wore baggy clothes that camouflaged my ribs and bones. I asked for lunch money each week even though I never used it. I was a genius at making up new excuses, and I lied when I was confronted about not eating. Besides, how could anything be wrong with me if I was maintaining a 4.0 grade point and excelled in every activity I possibly could at school? I appeared perfect on the outside, but I was crying for help on the inside.

I was very confused. I knew I was starving myself even though I didn't want to admit it at the time. I knew that what I was doing was wrong and was harmful to my body, but I also honestly believed that the more weight I lost, the happier, healthier, and better off I would be. I was addicted to losing weight. I couldn't stop. I would tell myself that I would stop when I got to a certain weight, but my weight just never got low enough to meet my standards. I'd tell myself that I could do better and just lose five more pounds. . . .

I Hate My Weight

STORY—PAGE 2

I felt tremendous guilt lying to my family, but I couldn't help it. I felt awful that I was always a pain to be around, but I put my eating disorder ahead of everything, including family and friends. I was ashamed of myself but, at the same time, proud. No one else at school had my willpower. I always got this incredible high when watching others eat while I sat and ate nothing. I felt like I had power and control and was getting attention. I thought starving myself was the only thing I was good at, despite the fact that I did well in everything. But like everything else in my life, I had to excel at starving; I had to be the best. Unfortunately, the best also meant feeling the worst. But I was determined to be the thinnest girl in school. Just hearing about someone who weighed less than me shot jealousy up my spine. I thought if I were the thinnest, I'd be popular, have boyfriends, and definitely make the cheerleading squad.

As my weight dropped, my parents became very concerned. I went from doctor to doctor, and saw dietitians and therapists. But no one could do anything to help me because I didn't want help, and I didn't believe anything was wrong with me. Finally, when I got to my lowest weight (4 feet, 10 inches–55 pounds), my parents and therapist told me I had to be hospitalized. They pulled me out of school by surprise, and I cried all the way to the hospital. They had threatened to do this before if I didn't gain weight on my own, but I never took them seriously. I was mad and really scared. I still thought I was fine.

The first weeks of treatment were the worst days of my life, but now I look back and thank God I was forced to go there. When the doctor said he'd do everything possible to save my life, I knew I was where I had to be. But I still didn't want to get better. I restricted my food and tried to get away with everything I could. I threw food away or hid it in my napkin. I cried myself to sleep every night. The only positive thing about treatment was talking to other girls with eating disorders. I learned I was not the only one who had these strange thoughts about food. I wasn't the only one who believed one little bite of anything would make me gain 10 pounds. I wasn't the only one who knew the exact amount of fat and calories in every food imaginable. I wasn't the only one who saw myself as overweight when my ribs protruded out of my body. I wasn't the only one who was afraid to eat in front of others or who was terrified about any situation having to do with food. I wasn't the only one who paid attention to everything everyone else ate.

I Hate My Weight

STORY—PAGE 3

Frustrated with all the restrictions at the hospital, I finally gave treatment a chance. By refusing to eat my meals, I would just have to stay longer. They threatened to feed me intravenously since I was so dangerously thin, so I figured that if I had to gain weight, I might as well gain it by eating real food. First I had to admit to myself that I was anorexic and needed help. Then I started eating meals and attending classes on self-esteem, sexuality, nutrition, communication, and body image. From group therapy I learned that my eating disorder was just a symptom, and underneath was my problem with perfectionism.

After I had been in treatment for about a month, I was able to convince everybody, including myself, that I was better. On weekend passes I ate perfectly. I complied with treatment. They discharged me before I'd reached my ideal weight. I was scared about being on my own. Treatment had been a safe place, and now eating would be my responsibility again.

I did fine until school started in the fall. I got very busy, and this created stress. Practicing my eating disorder was the only way I knew to relieve stress, so that's what I did until it finally caught up with me in my sophomore year. That year I had to be hospitalized again. I was angry. I had promised myself I wouldn't relapse. I had failed myself and my family. I had let everyone down. I didn't want to be anorexic anymore, but at the same time, I didn't want to give it up. Who was I without it? I had been this way since third grade. What would life be without an eating disorder? I wasn't ready to let it go since it was what was so familiar to me, but at the same time, I wanted to.

Treatment didn't help much during my sophomore year, and my junior year of high school was even worse. In addition to my eating disorder, I'd become very depressed and obsessive. I didn't want to wake up in the morning, and I could barely make it through a day at school. I fell asleep every hour. Teachers were calling my parents, and everyone was upset with me. I was restricting myself to a cup of rice and a bottle of water a day. I would only allow myself to eat that after I had finished the laundry and other things on my list. I couldn't eat until I had done my daily exercise routine, which consisted of a 3- to 5-mile run, 40 minutes on the stair machine, 40 minutes on the exercise bike, and 1,600 sit-ups. I don't know how I was able to run on calories I didn't even have. I invented new rules for myself. I only deserved to eat if I had

I Hate My Weight

STORY—PAGE 4

accomplished what I considered to be a lot. I became stricter and stricter. It got to the point where it would be 11:00 P.M. and I still hadn't eaten once that day because I didn't have enough chores done yet. I had to wash my dishes–even if they had already been washed in the dishwasher–shower, and vacuum the house before I felt like things were clean enough for me to eat.

Things continued to get worse. Once I went for 48 hours without eating a thing. I learned how to ignore hunger. Sometimes even collapsing on the ground wasn't enough to prove to myself that I needed food and rest. Then whenever I did give in and eat, I felt tremendous guilt. I thought I was a pig that didn't deserve to be fed, so I exercised as much as I could to get it off.

I was able to keep this up for three months. But I had lost 15 pounds and was admitted to the hospital again. This time I wanted to go back and I wanted to get better, but I knew I couldn't do it on my own. I knew this time that I had to get better for myself, not for my parents or doctors. I got more out of this treatment than my first two combined. I was finally ready to change my old, safe habits. I couldn't go on living an anorexic life, if you could call that a life. I struggled with the fact that I was now, in addition to being diagnosed with an eating disorder, labeled as depressive and obsessive-compulsive. Now I was even weirder than I thought. Now I had three disorders to fight. I thought I was a nut case, especially when my doctors put me on Prozac. But I had to admit that I needed help and I had to be willing to accept it.

I have gotten much better since that hospitalization. I have stopped rewashing dishes and showering every time before I eat. I can vacuum only once a day and go for an entire week without dusting the house. It no longer takes me 30 minutes in the produce aisle to pick out the best apple. I can eat before I go to work and at school. Since I started taking Prozac I am not depressed. I can be with my friends and have fun. I have energy to do things. Now I weigh more than I ever have, but I also feel better than I can ever remember.

Food and weight are still big issues for me, but now it's more important for me to be happy than it is to be thin. I know I want to recover, so I might as well start now. I look forward to each day now, and although each meal is still a struggle, I'm just taking it one meal at a time.

I Hate My Weight

STORY—PAGE 5

Recently I learned that one of my friends who was in treatment with me died from anorexia. She was 12 years old. That made me realize how stupid I have been. I regret what I have done. I regret what I have done to my body. I won't be able to have children because I never started getting my period. I starved myself for so long that my cholesterol level is extremely high. I won't ever get taller because I starved myself during my growth spurt. I wish I had never had an eating disorder, but I've learned and grown a lot from it. My mistakes have made me a stronger person, but it's a big price to pay. I'm mad at society for creating an unrealistic ideal body image for women. I still sometimes wish I were that anorexic girl again when I see anyone skinnier than me, but I know that I can't be happy and practice an eating disorder at the same time. I have to choose between the two, and I have finally decided on happiness.

Until this year I've kept my eating disorder a secret as much as possible, but I'm tired of living a superficial life. I can't go on pretending to be someone I'm not. I'm Cara, not anorexic Cara. My friends and family like the real me more, and so do I.

Having an eating disorder is not as glamorous as it appears. It is like being addicted to drugs. You want to stop, but you can't. It gives you a high but, at the same time, a down that you can't even see. You are in denial until things get to their worst point and you scare yourself to death. Food controls you; it becomes your life. Everything you do revolves around food, and you are like an addict . . . you do whatever it takes to practice. Everything else comes last.

—Cara, Age 17

Living Up to an Image

Developmental Perspective

This period of development can be a struggle for adolescents as they try to figure out who they really are or attempt to live up to the way they think others see them. They may have difficulty breaking free of the images others have of them, even if the images no longer reflect how they see themselves. Sometimes this tension results in alienation or feelings of guilt that they aren't living up to others' expectations.

Objectives

▷ To compare self-image with one's perceptions of how others see one

▷ To learn not to equate self-worth with others' perceptions of one

Materials

▷ Paper and pencil for each student

▷ A large, two-sided mirror. On one side of the mirror, tape individual slips of paper with the following words: *lazy, unmotivated, rebellious, cocky.* On the other side, tape individual slips of paper with the following words: *bored, sick of school, sick of rules, sure of myself.*

▷ A copy of the Living Up to an Image–Poem (Handout 5) for each student

▷ Construction paper, glue, scissors, markers, magazines, and other art materials

Procedure

1. Introduce the lesson by asking each student to think about two important people in his or her life, identify them by name on a sheet of paper, and then write two or three words to describe how he or she thinks each person sees him or her. In other words, have students ask themselves, "What is that person's image of me?" The answer for a close friend might be "intelligent and fun-loving"; for a parent, "confident and responsible."

2. Invite students to share their responses with a partner. As a group, discuss whether or not the images other people have of the students correspond to their self-images. Ask them if they ever feel they are letting someone down because the way others see them isn't the way they see themselves. Give examples, such as thinking that one's parents see one as a confident musician but inwardly having lots of doubts about one's ability to perform or thinking that one's grandparents see one as a sweet, innocent teenager when one has experienced more than they know.

3. Discuss the fact that sometimes it is easy to entertain self-doubt and begin to feel worthless when others' perceptions of one are negative or when there is a discrepancy in perceptions. Hold up the two-sided mirror. Read the words on the first side, which represent someone else's perception. Then read the words on the other side. Ask students if the person described is a bad person if others see him or her in a negative light. Emphasize the fact that they are fallible human beings, and stress that, regardless of how others perceive them or how they perceive themselves, they need to accept themselves as worthwhile individuals even if they have faults or see themselves differently than others see them.

4. Distribute a copy of the Living Up to an Image–Poem (Handout 5) to each student to read.

5. Distribute the art materials and have students make collages representing images of themselves. Each student should divide a piece of construction paper in half, using one half to depict self-image and the other half to depict the way they think other significant people perceive them.

6. Allow time for students to share their collages in small groups, and then discuss the Content and Personalization Questions.

Discussion

CONTENT QUESTIONS

1. What do you think the teenager who wrote the poem meant about letting others down?

2. What do you think the writer of the poem meant by "going through the motions"?

3. What do you think the writer meant about feeling alone and empty? Why did he think no one noticed?

PERSONALIZATION QUESTIONS

1. Can you identify in any way with the message in this poem? (Invite sharing.)

2. When you made your collage, was your image of yourself the same as or different from the image you think others have of you?

3. The teenager who wrote the poem seemed to be struggling with feelings about not living up to the images of others. Is this true for you as well? If so, how do you deal with this?

4. If you are not living up to another person's image of you, are you worthless? What do you need to remember so you don't put yourself down?

Follow-up Activity

Encourage students to write their own poems or stories about their self-images and how they think others see them.

Living Up to an Image

POEM

I've let down my family, my friends, and the pure innocent child
that once existed within me.

Oh, the young child I used to be, without a trace of guilt or sin
upon my soul.

I often question myself about what still exists of me.

Years go by; each one comes and goes faster than the previous.

And with each year comes something so strong, so unfamiliar
to my childhood.

Who am I? I no longer know.

They say they don't expect me to live up to others, but I sense
the disappointment

When I don't follow in their footsteps. But is that me?
I don't think so . . .

I'm not who they think I am.

Can't they see how alone I am? Can't they see the empty
look in my eyes?

Can't they notice or even care that the little child they once
knew isn't even there?

Can't they see how I'm going through the motions, but my heart
and soul aren't there?

I want you to know me; I want you to care. But how can I do
that when the me I see is

Not the me you think is me?

—Alex, Age 16

Changing Feelings

Developmental Perspective

Adolescents are easily overwhelmed by the frequency and intensity of their negative emotions. They often feel powerless to do anything about those emotions. In order to prevent these feelings from dominating their lives, it is important to help them identify specific ways to deal effectively with negative emotions.

Objective

▷ To identify specific ways to change negative feelings

Materials

▷ A Changing Feelings–Worksheet (Handout 6) and a pencil for each student

Procedure

1. Introduce the lesson by explaining the objective. Next, distribute the Changing Feelings–Worksheet (Handout 6) to each student, and ask students to read it. Before having them complete the practice activity at the end of the handout, spend time reviewing the concepts that are explained.

2. Ask students to complete the examples at the end of the worksheet and discuss their responses with a partner.

3. Discuss the Content and Personalization Questions.

Discussion

CONTENT QUESTIONS

1. Explain what irrational beliefs are, and give examples.

2. What does it mean to "dispute"?

3. How can feelings change if thoughts change?

PERSONALIZATION QUESTIONS

1. Do you ever have any irrational thoughts? (Invite sharing.)

2. Have you ever tried to dispute your irrational thoughts? If so, what does that do to your feelings?

3. How do you think you can apply the information from this activity to your life?

Follow-up Activity

Have students monitor their thoughts and feelings for several days and then share examples of irrational beliefs/and or the effects of their attempts to dispute irrational beliefs.

Changing Feelings

WORKSHEET–PAGE 1

Name: _____ Date: _____

Instructions: Read the following explanation, then complete the examples at the end of the worksheet. Discuss your examples with a partner.

According to Albert Ellis, who developed Rational-Emotive Behavior Therapy, people don't have to stay miserable, unhappy, upset, depressed, angry, guilty, or ashamed. Of course, it's not quite as easy as waving a magic wand, but you can change your feelings if you change the way you think about things. Here's how you do it:

► First, you identify an upsetting situation or an event . . . something that you did or something that happened to you. We call this the activating event *(A)*.

► Next, you identify how you are feeling about this event or situation. This is called the emotional consequence *(C)*.

► Next, you need to remember that these feelings don't just happen. Someone else could have felt entirely differently about this same event. Therefore, you look at what you are thinking that results in these feelings. There are three types of thinking that can create negative feelings. We call these types of thinking *irrational beliefs*. Irrational beliefs include the following:

Self-downing: This means that whenever something happens, you immediately think that it is your fault or that you are a bad person. You equate your self-worth with your performance. For example, if you get a bad grade, you think you are a rotten person. People who engage in self-downing have trouble accepting criticism. They think that they have to be perfect and that if they aren't, they are bad people.

Demanding: When you demand that everything go your way and be fair, and you think that it is awful if it isn't, you are setting yourself up for big-time anger. Not everything in the world is fair, and you can't make everyone do exactly as you wish all the time. You can control only yourself, not others.

Low frustration tolerance: This means that you think everything should come easily to you, that you shouldn't have to work too hard for anything, and that if something is boring, you shouldn't have to do it.

In addition, awfulizing, overgeneralizing, and making assumptions are forms of irrational thinking. When you awfulize, overgeneralize, or make assumptions, you make a situation much worse than it really is. You assume things without ever checking out the facts, you think things will never get better, and you just think everything is awful.

Changing Feelings

WORKSHEET—PAGE 2

► Once you have identified your irrational beliefs *(B),* then you dispute them *(D).* You do this by finding evidence or asking yourself some critical questions. The following example, concerning 14-year-old Ashlie, will help you understand the A-B-C-D process.

Ashlie is in junior high. She has lots of friends, but she often fights with them. She also has a boyfriend, but she fights a lot with him, too. Here's what happened with Ashlie recently:

A = Ashlie's boyfriend said he'd meet her at the mall, but he never showed up.

C = Ashlie felt angry at first, and then she started feeling depressed.

B = Ashlie had these thoughts:

> Demanding: He said he would come, so he should have. There's no excuse.
>
> Awfulizing/overgeneralizing: He never does what he says he will. He's always unreliable. I really had counted on seeing him, and it's awful that he didn't show up because now I won't get to see him until Monday. He's probably over at Anna's house and just stood me up.
>
> Low frustration tolerance: I can't stand this. He shouldn't make my life so miserable.
>
> Self-downing: He probably likes someone better than me. I probably ticked him off by something I did. Maybe I'm just not hot enough for him, or something.

D = Ashlie disputed her thoughts in this way:

> I can demand all I want, but my boyfriend will do what he wants. I can't control him, so why make myself angry because he isn't here? There's no law that says he has to be. Just because he's not here, does that necessarily mean he's with Anna? And is he never reliable? Haven't there been any times that he's done what he said he'd do? I can stand it, even if I don't like it. The fact that he didn't show up doesn't mean he likes someone else better than me. And the fact that he didn't show up doesn't necessarily mean that I did something to tick him off or that I'm not good enough for him.

Changing Feelings

WORKSHEET–PAGE 3

If you ask yourself questions like Ashlie did, you get a clearer picture of the real issues and are likely to be less upset. This process of disputing is a good way for you to challenge your thinking and feel less emotionally upset. It doesn't guarantee you will be happy, but you will probably be less angry–maybe just irritated. Remember, when you are really angry, you can't problem solve very effectively, and when you continually put yourself down and assume that you are not good enough or that everything is your fault, you become depressed. These aren't emotions that teenagers usually like to have, so if you want to help yourself feel less negative, try this A-B-C-D process.

Practice now with an example from your life. Remember that you need to use this process only when you have negative feelings. When you are feeling positive, you won't have these beliefs that cause problems and result in bad feelings.

Example 1

A (event): _____

C (feelings): _____

B (beliefs): _____

D (disputes): _____

Example 2

A (event): _____

C (feelings): _____

B (beliefs): _____

D (disputes): _____

Controlling Confusion

Developmental Perspective

Although at this point adolescents are generally beginning to experience increasing emotional stability, this depends on when they entered puberty. Furthermore, as they enter this stage of development, they are confronted with numerous issues that result in confusion: relationships and sexuality, future plans, and insecurities about their abilities. This confusion is often very troubling, and it is important to help adolescents learn to deal with it instead of resorting to self-defeating behaviors.

Objectives

▷ To identify sources of confusion

▷ To learn effective strategies for dealing with confusion

Materials

▷ A copy of the Controlling Confusion–Checklist (Handout 7) and the Controlling Confusion–Solutions (Handout 8) for each student

▷ A pencil for each student

Procedure

1. Introduce the activity by asking each student to think quickly of one thing that is confusing for him or her as an adolescent. Invite sharing.

2. Distribute the Controlling Confusion–Checklist (Handout 7) to each student. Ask students to complete the checklist and add items that are confusing to them.

3. Following completion of the checklist, have students discuss their responses with a partner.

4. Distribute the Controlling Confusion–Solutions (Handout 8) to each student. Ask students to read the suggestions, add their own, and then circle the ones they have used. Have pairs of students join other pairs and, in groups of four, discuss reactions to the solutions handout.

5. Discuss the Content and Personalization Questions.

Discussion

CONTENT QUESTIONS

1. Was it difficult to assign the ratings on the checklist? If so, what made it difficult?

2. What other sources of confusion did you add to the checklist?

3. Were you aware of all of the solutions identified in the handout? If not, which ones were new ideas for you? What's your opinion of the identified solutions?

4. After reading the list of solutions, were you able to identify others? (Invite sharing.)

PERSONALIZATION QUESTIONS

1. Did you identify with many of the items listed on the checklist?

2. How do you cope with your confusion? Do you think your methods are healthy or unhealthy?

3. If your coping methods are unhealthy, do you want to change them? If so, what is one thing you will do?

4. Are there solutions you learned about in this activity that make sense for you to try? If so, which ones?

Follow-up Activity

Ask students to write short essays about their confusion and how they deal with it. Also encourage them to add to their lists of solutions for coping with confusion and try the ideas suggested in the activity.

Controlling Confusion

CHECKLIST

Name: _____ Date: _____

Instructions: Read the items on the checklist, and respond to each item using a rating of 3 = a lot like me, 2 = somewhat like me, and 1 = not like me. Discuss your results with a partner.

_____ 1. I get angry for no apparent reason.

_____ 2. I think that no one else feels the same way I do.

_____ 3. I don't understand why I sometimes feel so guilty about the things I do.

_____ 4. I feel embarrassed a lot.

_____ 5. I feel mixed up about what I want to do with my life.

_____ 6. Growing up can be painful.

_____ 7. I don't know who I really am.

_____ 8. My mood swings confuse me.

_____ 9. I can't remember what it's like just to be happy and carefree most of the time.

_____ 10. Some of the things I think about scare me or confuse me (for example, wanting to be sexual, or thinking about ending my life even though I would never do it).

Controlling Confusion

SOLUTIONS

1. Realize that you are not alone; most teenagers feel some degree of confusion about growing up.

2. Don't act impulsively. In other words, even though you may feel very depressed, remember that this depression won't last forever. Don't think about throwing yourself off the bridge because you can't stand the pain. The pain is only temporary.

3. Develop tolerance for frustration. Remind yourself that life isn't always easy; that some things are boring; and that most people have to work at things if they want to succeed, get ahead, or feel better. Don't just give up because something is too hard.

4. Talk to people about your confusion. Don't be afraid to express how you really feel. If you don't think your parents will understand, ask them to hook you up with a counselor. To find a good one, check with some of your friends who also go to counseling to see who really understands teenagers. Remember, you are not crazy if you see a counselor because you feel bad. Wouldn't you see a medical doctor if you felt bad physically? It's really no different.

5. Don't hang around with kids who are looking for trouble and who may make stupid decisions as a result. Sometimes that will just bring you down even more.

6. Think twice about using drugs and alcohol to help yourself feel better. In the long run, this will just create a new set of problems.

7. Try writing songs, poetry, or journal entries to help you get your feelings out. Then think about sharing what you write with someone who can help you sort through the confusion.

8. Take things a day at a time. The older you get, the more likely it is that you will feel less confused. Don't give up; adolescence doesn't last forever.

9. Learn to think rationally. Check out your assumptions; don't put yourself down. Have preferences instead of making demands.

10. Realize that these kinds of thoughts are normal at your age. If you are really worried, talk to someone you trust.

Add your suggestions:

11. _____

_____

_____

12. _____

_____

_____

Peeling Away the Layers

Developmental Perspective

Although adolescents at this stage are becoming increasingly adept at expressing their emotions, it is still very common to see anger mask other feelings such as hurt, pain, depression, or ambivalence. These feelings, which generally are at the core of the real problems, often go unaddressed because the focus is on the anger. Helping adolescents understand the feelings they cover up is an important part of their emotional development process.

Objectives

▷ To learn about the concept of covering up feelings

▷ To identify the positive and negative effects of covering up feelings

Materials

▷ An onion and a knife

▷ Paper and pencil for each student

▷ A copy of the Peeling Away the Layers–Situations (Handout 9) for each student

Procedure

1. Introduce the activity by displaying an onion and slowly peeling it, asking students to watch and comment on what is happening. Note that onions have layers that can be peeled away.

2. Discuss the fact that there are often layers to our feelings. In other words, a person may actually feel hurt or depressed but cover that feeling up with anger or a smile. Discuss with students the reasons they might try to cover up their real feelings and the advantages and disadvantages of doing this.

3. Ask each student to take out a sheet of paper and fold it into 1-inch accordion folds. Distribute the Peeling Away the Layers–Situations (Handout 9) to each student. As students read Situation 1, each one should write a number 1 on the first fold of paper and write down the first word that describes the most obvious feeling represented in that situation. Then, on the next several folds, students should identify other feelings that might have been covered up by the first feeling. After students have processed the first situation, have them write the number 2 on a slip, read Situation 2, and respond as before.

4. When students have finished responding, have them form triads to discuss the situations and the feelings they identified.

5. Discuss the Content and Personalization Questions.

Discussion

CONTENT QUESTIONS

1. Was it difficult to find words to identify the feelings described or implied in the situations?

2. Did you and other members of your small group agree on the feelings?

3. What does the concept of peeling away the layers mean? Do you think this is something that people do frequently?

PERSONALIZATION QUESTIONS

1. Have you ever covered up your feelings with anger, a smile, or some other emotion? If so, what was your reason for doing it?

2. Do you think it is easier to help yourself deal with real feelings if you cover them up? Why or why not?

3. Do you think covering up your feelings is good? Why or why not?

4. What did you learn about feelings from this activity?

Follow-up Activity

Have students write or find poems that illustrate the concept of covering up feelings and peeling the layers away.

Peeling Away the Layers

SITUATIONS

Name: _____ Date: _____

Instructions: Read Situation 1. Then write a number 1 on the first fold of your paper, and write down the first feeling you notice in the situation. Then, on the next folds, write the other feelings that are covered up by the first one. Repeat the process for Situation 2.

Situation 1

I was reading something in a magazine that said, "Some people are laughing on the outside, but they are sad and crying on the inside." That describes me. I wake up and put on a smile and act the part all day. It's hard. Sometimes I'll be standing at my locker and see people whispering. I just smile and walk on by, but I think they are talking about me when I got drunk and was making out at the party. I can't let them know how I really feel. When I come home from school I sometimes can't keep on acting; I just take my feelings out on my parents.

Situation 2

I don't know why I act the way I do sometimes. I was at a party, and I guess I wanted my girlfriend's attention. She kept talking to other people, so I'd just start acting really stupid and crazy to try to get her to notice me. Then she went outside with some guy, and I just lost it. I saw them inside the car, and I thought they were making out. I was just going to go tap on the window, but I must have been stronger than I thought, and I broke the window. I couldn't face anyone, so I just ran away, and then later that night I went home.

Will I Ever Feel Better?

Developmental Perspective

Adolescents think in the here and now. Everything seems very immediate to them, and they have trouble projecting into the future. When they are overwhelmed with negative emotions–many of which they don't understand–it is very easy for them to assume that their anger, depression, or confusion will last forever. This is of concern as young people at this age do contemplate suicide because they can't stand the thought of feeling this bad forever. Helping them understand that the negative feelings are probably temporary is very important in helping them deal more effectively with the present.

Objective

▷ To develop perspective on emotional turmoil

Materials

▷ A copy of the Will I Ever Feel Better? Story (Handout 10) for each student

Procedure

1. After explaining the lesson objective, distribute a copy of the Will I Ever Feel Better? Story (Handout 10) to each student. Invite students to read the story silently and write short reactions at the bottom of the handout.

2. After students have finished reading and writing their reactions, discuss the Content and Personalization Questions.

Discussion

CONTENT QUESTIONS

1. How did the teenager in the story feel when she was 14? Now that she is 16, are her negative feelings as bad?

2. Were there specific situations that upset Kathie, or did she just feel bad in general?

3. What happened to change Kathie's feelings?

PERSONALIZATION QUESTIONS

1. Have you had an experience similar to Kathie's?

2. Does it help you to know that negative feelings probably won't last forever?

3. How has the information presented today been useful to you?

Follow-up Activity

Invite several older students to address the group about intense feelings and whether the feelings have become less intense as they have grown older.

Will I Ever Feel Better?

STORY—PAGE 1

Name: _____ Date: _____

Instructions: Read this true story. Then write a few sentences expressing your reactions at the bottom of this handout.

I was 14 when I first started to feel depressed. There wasn't anything in particular going on in my life that I was feeling bad about. I had good friends, I got along pretty well with my parents, and I did well in school. Sometimes I fought with my younger sister, but that wasn't the cause of the bad feelings. I could just be sitting in class or hanging out in the lunchroom and I would suddenly feel down. Sometimes those moods would last for the rest of the day, and sometimes I would feel better the next hour. It was confusing.

What made matters worse is that when I felt this way, I sometimes just wanted to snap people's heads off. I'd talk back to my parents for no reason, and they'd get on my case. Or I sometimes went off on my friends. That was really embarrassing, and I didn't understand why I did it. My parents finally decided to have me see a counselor. At first I was really upset about that, and I told them I wasn't going to say anything. I thought that they must think I was crazy because they were making me go. But I had no choice. During the first session, the counselor told me that she understood that I might not like coming to counseling because I might think there was something really wrong with me. The counselor said that she didn't think that was the case based on what she had learned from my parents, and she explained that feeling depressed and angry during early adolescence is very normal. I felt relieved when she said that, but I still wasn't about to say much to this person. The counselor gave me some information about how long this moodiness could last. She suggested that it might go on for several months or up to a year, but that it wouldn't last forever unless it was a chemically based depression, in which case medication could help. She told me she could help me find some ways to manage these moods if I was willing.

I left the first session feeling a little better. At least I knew that I was normal and that I wasn't the only kid who felt this way. I also was glad to know this wouldn't last the rest of my life. I still wasn't all that convinced that anyone could help me manage these moods better. But I figured I might as well give it a try since I had to go. Anything would be better than feeling like I did. During the second session I did tell the counselor a little bit more about how I was feeling. I mentioned that when I got depressed, it just seemed like everything was awful. The counselor helped me learn to put things in perspective by showing me a catastrophe scale. This is a way of rating from 1 to 10 how bad

Will I Ever Feel Better?

STORY–PAGE 2

things really are. She also suggested that I make a list of things that I liked to do or that helped me feel better so I could refer to this list and try something when the bad moods started. She told me that I might have to force myself to do something to get out of the mood rather than just allow it to keep on developing. I told her this would be hard because sometimes when I felt bad, all I wanted to do was sleep. The counselor told me that was normal, but she said that it is better to stay active because then it is harder to feel depressed. She also told me that some of her other clients said writing in journals, listening to music, or drawing helped them deal with depression.

I continued to see the counselor for a while, and my moods did start to improve. Now I am 16 and much less depressed. I don't get irritated as often, and although I still have bad times, they aren't as frequent as they used to be. Now if I get depressed I don't think it will last forever, and I know I'm not crazy. Just recently I noticed that my 13-year-old sister is starting to act the same way I did when I was 14. I heard my mother tell my sister that it was just adolescence . . . and that she'd outgrow it. I think that's what happened with me.

–Kathie, Age 16

Rumors & Relationships

Developmental Perspective

Although at this stage many adolescents are beginning to think more abstractly, a development implying the ability to consider multiple points of view in assessing relationship issues, many are still immature in the ways they communicate with others. Rumors, gossip, and unfounded assumptions can result in many interpersonal relationship difficulties during adolescence.

Objectives

▷ To identify the negative impact of rumors, gossip, and assumptions

▷ To learn ways to stop the negative cycle of rumors, gossip, and assumptions

Materials

▷ Paper and pencil for each student

▷ A slip of paper with the following message printed on it:

> You wouldn't believe what that teacher told Isaiah. She told him that if he didn't get his grades up, she would make sure he didn't play football and that she would phone his parents and tell them he shouldn't get to go out during the week at all. She also threatened to tell Isaiah's girlfriend that she couldn't see him either until things improved, not just in her class, but in all classes. The teacher told him that every single teacher in this school thinks he is the laziest student here.

Procedure

1. Introduce the lesson by asking for eight volunteers, who should stand in a line at the front of the room. Take the first volunteer aside, and tell him or her the message. Then have that person tell the next, and so on down the line. Ask the person at the end to say the message out loud, and compare it to the original as you read it.

2. Debrief the stimulus activity by discussing the concept of rumors and gossip and considering how a message can so easily be distorted as it is passed from one person to the next. Ask students how common rumors and gossip are for their age group and how they affect relationships.

3. Ask students to take out paper and pencil and respond in writing to the following:

   ▶ First, identify a time when you have been the object of a rumor or gossip (or have been part of the process in some way).

   ▶ Second, identify how you felt when that happened.

> ► Third, identify what you were telling yourself about the rumor or gossip: Were you what the gossipers said you were?
>
> ► Fourth, identify the consequences of the rumor or gossip.

4. Ask students to find partners and discuss what they wrote. In the total group, discuss feelings associated with rumors and gossip, including the consequences. Introduce the concept of jumping to conclusions–assuming things without checking out the facts. Ask students to comment on the way this practice relates to rumors and gossip and its negative impact on relationships. Describe the following negative cycle of interaction to illustrate how behaviors are impacted by listening to rumors:

> ► Student 1 hears a rumor about him- or herself.
>
> ► Student 1 reacts to the rumor by getting upset.
>
> ► Student 2 reacts to Student 1's behavior.
>
> ► Student 1 reacts to Student 2's behavior.
>
> ► And so on . . . until someone breaks the cycle.

5. Teach students to stop the negative cycle. To do so, they first need to ask themselves if what others are saying about them is true. If it isn't, is it worth getting upset about? Can they control what others say or do? Second, they need to check out the facts before acting on assumptions. Illustrate with the following example:

> Josie was walking down the school corridor, and she ran into Amy. She asked Amy if Amy had seen her boyfriend, Peter. Amy replied, "Yes, but I don't think you'll want to find him right now. He's in the lunchroom with Cara." Josie immediately assumed that Peter didn't like her anymore and that he had been out with Cara the night before since he hadn't been with her. Josie waited until after school, and then she confronted Peter, saying, "I know you were with Cara last night. Just forget you ever knew me. I don't want anything to do with you." She threw his letter jacket and ring in his face and raced off to the parking lot. Peter yelled after her, "If that's the way you want to be, I want you out of my life, too."

> Ask students what they know to be true in this situation. Discuss how Josie's assumptions affected her behavior, which in turn affected Peter's. Refer to the negative cycle of interaction, and invite students to comment on how this cycle could have been different if Josie hadn't made assumptions.

6. Discuss the Content and Personalization Questions.

Discussion

CONTENT QUESTIONS

1. Do you think rumors, gossip, and assumptions are common in relationships among teens? If so, how do these things affect relationships? Is the impact positive or negative?

2. What can be done to stop the negative cycle of interaction when people jump to conclusions or listen to gossip and rumors?

PERSONALIZATION QUESTIONS

1. Have you been affected by gossip, rumors, or jumping to conclusions? If so, what was the impact on your relationships?

2. If you hear others gossiping about you, do you stop to question whether what they say is true? If it isn't, how does getting upset help? Even if what others say is true, does that mean you aren't a good person?

3. Would you like to do anything to change the way you jump to conclusions or "buy into" rumors and gossip? If so, what would you like to change, and how can you do it?

Follow-up Activity

Ask students to implement the concept of checking out facts in order to avoid the negative cycle of interaction, which results in relationships characterized by rumors and gossip. Have them write short reports on the effects of checking out the facts.

Heartbreak & a Half

Developmental Perspective

Although some teenagers start dating earlier, more serious relationships with deeper emotional involvement don't usually begin until after age 15. Even though they are more mature now than they were in middle school, adolescents' ability to deal with intense relationships depends to a large extent on individual level of abstract thinking and emotional maturity.

Objectives

▷ To examine feelings and issues involved in the termination of a romantic relationship

▷ To explore effective ways to deal with the termination of a relationship

▷ To recognize that the breakup of a romantic relationship does not reflect on one's worth as a person

Materials

▷ A chalkboard

▷ Paper and pencil for each student

▷ Four sheets of newsprint, each marked with one of the following words: *anger, depression, guilt, hurt*

▷ Four blank sheets of newsprint and a marker per group of students

▷ A copy of the Heartbreak and a Half–Story (Handout 11) for each student

▷ A copy of the Heartbreak and a Half–Essay (Handout 12) for each student (for the Follow-up Activity)

Procedure

1. Introduce the lesson by asking each student to take out paper and pencil and quickly brainstorm a list of feelings that he or she thinks are associated with the breakup of a romantic relationship. List the terms on the board. Then discuss the ways relationships end, such as the following: breakup initiated by one party, and the other one doesn't want the relationship to end; breakup initiated by one or both parties, with mutual agreement; breakup initiated impulsively as a result of an argument; or breakup occurring on parents' orders. Discuss whether the feelings and thoughts are the same in each of these cases or whether they vary depending on the circumstance.

2. Post the four sheets of newsprint with feeling words. Divide students into four groups, and assign one of these words to each group. Give each group a blank sheet of newsprint and a marker, and instruct them to write down thoughts associated with the feeling word. For example, if the word is *guilt,* the thought

might be "I should have tried harder to make the relationship work." Then ask each group to share results with the total group. Emphasize the connections between particular feelings and thought patterns: Anger is often associated with thinking that another person shouldn't have acted as he or she did. Depression is associated with thinking that a situation is awful, that one can't imagine going on without a certain relationship, or that there is something wrong with one because the relationship didn't work out. Guilt is associated with thinking one should have done something differently, and frustration is associated with the thought that one can't stand the discomfort and that the relationship shouldn't be so difficult to deal with.

3. Distribute a copy of the Heartbreak and a Half–Story (Handout 11) to each student. Have students read the story and respond to the questions at the end.

4. Have students form groups of four to discuss their reactions to the story and their responses to the questions.

5. Discuss the Content and Personalization Questions.

Discussion

CONTENT QUESTIONS

1. Do you think the experience of the teenager in the story is typical for students your age? Why or why not?

2. What did you think about the way she was coping with the breakup? What additional suggestions do you have for dealing with her situation in a healthy way?

3. If someone breaks up with you, are you worthless?

4. If someone breaks up with you, even though it seems bad, can you stand it? Do you think you will eventually feel better, and if so, what can you do to help yourself get over the bad feelings?

5. Do you think it makes a difference in how you feel and what you think if you are the one to end the relationship instead of the other person? Why or why not?

PERSONALIZATION QUESTIONS

1. Have you ever experienced anything like the situation in the story? If so, how did you feel?

2. If you have been in a relationship that has ended, how did you cope with the breakup? Do you think you coped in healthy or unhealthy ways?

3. If you have been in a relationship that has ended, what about the breakup was especially difficult for you?

Follow-up Activity

Invite students to read the Heartbreak and a Half–Essay (Handout 12), then write stories or poems expressing how they have felt if they have been in relationships that have ended.

Heartbreak & a Half

STORY–PAGE 1

Name: _____ Date: _____

Instructions: Read this true story, and respond to the questions at the end.

Here it is . . . my story of trying to survive what I felt was a heartbreak and a half.

The first time I saw Shane, I thought he was a total nerd, always sitting so quietly in class. Then one weekend I realized that we hung out with the same crowd, and the more I looked at him, the more I wanted to know him. I started calling him, and we talked for about a month. Finally, he asked me out, and of course I said yes.

He was such a sweetheart. One weekend he was going out of town, and he bought me roses because he said he'd miss me. We'd been together two weeks then. I was so happy . . . no one had ever bought me roses. He always came over to my house during the week to see me, and on weekends we did things with our friends.

Shane's best friend was Travis, and mine was Angie. Angie was also a friend of Shane's, and they had had a short past. That didn't bother me because I felt like I had nothing to worry about. Everything went smoothly until one day I had Angie over and Shane and Travis came over. Angie was flirting with Shane. The next day I told her it made me mad. She denied doing anything, but I warned her to stay away.

Shane and I had been going out for almost two months when we started drifting apart. One weekend we barely spoke, and on Monday my heart sank when he gave me a note in the hallway. We hadn't talked in two days, and before I even read the note I started to cry. I knew what it said the moment he handed it to me. I went home from school early and read the note over and over, crying harder each time I read it. In the note he said that it wasn't my fault, but that it had to do with family problems and he just couldn't handle a relationship now. He said he was sorry and hoped we could still be friends.

For the next few days I couldn't even eat. I cried a lot until I didn't think there were any tears left. Then I started to feel a little better, and I was confident that I was handling it well until I talked to Travis. Travis told me that four days after Shane had broken up with me, Angie had written Shane a note saying that she sometimes thought of him as more than a friend. They were talking to each other, and I had had no idea.

Heartbreak & a Half

STORY–PAGE 2

I was furious with Angie. It was hard enough to deal with the breakup, but now I also had to deal with what my best friend had done. I still loved him, but now he's with her. That's the way it has been for four weeks now. Finally, I told her just to be with him because I knew that I didn't have a chance and I only wanted him to be happy. I wonder if anyone can even understand how hard it was to tell her that or how hard it is now to pretend I don't care about him anymore. It's hard to see him sitting across the room in class and know he's thinking about her and not me. It's really depressing to think that I don't mean a thing to him anymore.

The only things I can do now are to keep myself busy, give it time, and try to remind myself that it's over and he won't be back. That is still hard to believe; I can't accept the fact that even when his relationship with Angie is over he won't run back to me. I also write poems, which helps me indirectly say how I'm feeling. The weird thing is that the first week or two we were apart, all I did was cry, and now when I'm about to cry the tears won't come. It's like I don't have any left, or at least not for Shane. I'm trying my best to handle this, but it's so hard.

–Alicia, Age 15

1. What were some of the feelings Alicia experienced?

2. Why do you think Alicia was having so much difficulty handling this situation?

3. Was Alicia making any assumptions that might or might not have been true?

4. What did Alicia try to do to cope with this problem? Do you think these were good strategies?

Heartbreak & a Half

ESSAY

I am so overwhelmed by everything that I can't think straight. I don't know how I'll feel after today. I will miss him so much. I can't forget about him. I am really battling this, or at least I feel I am. Inside, my emotions are erupting from my warm blood. Deep inside I'm feeling empty, but at the same time I feel full because I have so much love for him. It is so difficult to explain how much I love him and how I shouldn't have any love for him. I just want to stand in his path so he can't leave me. These are emotions I shouldn't feel, but I do, and I can't seem to fight them. I'm not myself anymore like I wish I was. I'm not the same person I want to be. But I can't go back and change the unchangeable even though I wish I could. I think everybody else but me knows what I should do. Why can't I do what I feel when it feels so right?

–Katrina, Age 15

Growing Apart

Developmental Perspective

Depending on their rate of maturation, adolescents at this stage of development are becoming more independent and are less afraid to express their individuality than they were in middle school. Consequently, they are less dependent on conforming and being part of the crowd. As they mature and begin to think more about what is important to them, they may drift away from former friends as interests, behaviors, and values change.

Objectives

▷ To learn that friendships change as one matures

▷ To clarify what is important in a friendship

Materials

▷ A copy of the Growing Apart–Worksheet (Handout 13) for each student

▷ Pencil and paper for each student

Procedure

1. Introduce the lesson by asking each student to think of a close friend he or she had in grade school. Have students raise their hands if they are still friends with these people. Discuss the fact that as young people mature, relationships with both adults and peers change for a variety of reasons. Elicit from students what some of those reasons might be.

2. Distribute a copy of the Growing Apart–Worksheet (Handout 13) to each student. Ask students to fill in the information requested.

3. Have students form small groups and discuss their responses to the worksheet.

4. Discuss the Content and Personalization Questions.

Discussion

CONTENT QUESTIONS

1. What did you learn about your relationships from this activity?

2. What reasons did you identify for some of your relationships changing? (Invite sharing.)

PERSONALIZATION QUESTIONS

1. If most of your relationships have changed, how do you feel about this?

2. Do you think your relationships have changed more with peers or with adults?

Follow-up Activity

Invite students to write letters to individuals they no longer have relationships with, expressing how they feel about this fact and expressing other things they care to share about memories of the relationships. They may or may not choose to send the letters.

Growing Apart

WORKSHEET–PAGE 1

Name: _____ Date: _____

Instructions: Follow the directions and answer the questions in the different parts of the worksheet.

Write down the names of six people (peers and/or adults) you were close to: three when you were in elementary school and three when you were in middle school.

Elementary school   Middle school

_____   _____

_____   _____

_____   _____

If you are still very close to these people, put the number 1 beside their name(s). If you are still somewhat close to these people, put the number 2 beside their name(s). If you are not at all close to these people, put the number 3 beside their name(s).

Think about why you are no longer very close to the people you marked as 2's and 3's. Check any of the following that might be reasons why you are no longer as close.

_____ Our interests changed.

_____ I am not as dependent on them as I used to be.

_____ It isn't as cool to be close to adults as it was when I was young.

_____ They are into drugs and alcohol, and I'm not.

_____ They are jocks and I'm not.

_____ They spend most of their time with a boyfriend or a girlfriend.

_____ They are preps and I'm not.

_____ They are "dirts" and I'm not.

_____ They are nerds and I'm not.

_____ Our personalities clash.

_____ We like different kinds of music.

_____ We hang out with different crowds.

Growing Apart

WORKSHEET–PAGE 2

_____ I'm more of a loner and they like to be with crowds.

_____ We go to different schools.

_____ (Add your own) _____

_____

_____ (Add your own) _____

_____

If you are not close to the people you listed, how do you feel about it?

_____

_____

_____

_____

If you are still close to the people you listed, what do you think it is about these relationships that keeps you together?

_____

_____

_____

_____

Why Do They Treat Me like This?

Developmental Perspective

Although they are increasingly mature, adolescents at this stage nevertheless still struggle with friendship issues. Rejection by peers can be very common, and feelings of jealously may surface when a peer excels academically, athletically, or musically. Competition may be especially prevalent during the senior year, when adolescents begin to compete for scholarships and awards. Helping adolescents learn to deal with rejection and peer relationship issues is critical.

Objectives

▷ To identify feelings associated with rejection by peers

▷ To learn not to put yourself down if you are rejected by others

▷ To learn effective ways to deal with rejection

Materials

▷ A copy of the Why Do They Treat Me like This? Poem (Handout 14) and a pencil for each student

Procedure

1. Introduce the lesson by discussing the reasons peers reject one another and the feelings associated with this rejection.

2. Distribute the Why Do They Treat Me like This? Poem (Handout 14) to each student. Ask students to read the poem and respond to the questions at the end.

3. Have students find partners and discuss the poem and their responses to the questions.

4. Discuss the Content and Personalization Questions.

Discussion

CONTENT QUESTIONS

1. What did this poem mean to you? What issues do you think the writer was dealing with?

2. Why do you think others were treating the writer with disrespect?

3. How do you think the writer could deal with this situation in a healthy way?

4. Do you think the writer should think less of herself if others don't like her?

PERSONALIZATION QUESTIONS

1. If you have been rejected or treated cruelly by friends, how have you dealt with the situation?

2. What, if anything, do you think you could have done differently that would have made the situation better?

3. If you have been rejected by someone, have you put yourself down or considered yourself no good because that person didn't like you? Is it true that you are no good if someone rejects you or your behavior?

4. What advice would you give to someone else who is experiencing these kinds of problems with peers?

Follow-up Activity

Have students write "Dear Ann Landers" letters about problems they may be having with peers and write themselves responses suggesting ways to deal with the problems.

Why Do They Treat Me like This?

POEM–PAGE 1

Name: _____ Date: _____

Instructions: Read the poem, and respond to the questions at the end.

I didn't ask for much–

Only an answer.

Is that too much to ask for?

Why?

Why me?

Why am I the one who gets almost everyone I've cared for taken away or changed so I don't know the same people anymore?

Why me?

Why do all these people treat me with disregard and disrespect?

I know how our society is, yet they seem to be going beyond that in my case.

Don't they realize that people can take only so much before they feel like taking action?

Sometimes I think ending it all would just be easier, but if I did that, they would be winning.

That is something I can't allow–my hatred of them and their belief that I am worth nothing is what drives me.

Just wait–I'll prove them all wrong.

Then they will be the ones to suffer.

When I succeed they'll try to kiss up to me, but I'll just tell them to go to hell.

That's all they deserve.

The way they think they're superior, you'd think they were some version of a "superior race."

Why are they considered to be important when their parents are apparently influential? That doesn't make them better.

Why Do They Treat Me like This?

POEM—PAGE 2

I shouldn't hold grudges, but after the way they've treated me,
I can't seem to do anything but.

If someone else were in my shoes, they'd see.

They all think they know me—they are wrong.

They don't even have a clue.

Maybe someday if they get more mature, they might understand.

Understand why I am forced to act the way I do.

As they say, "It's lonely at the top."

More lonely than they'll ever know.

Why me?

—Allison, Age 16

1. What do you think this poem means?

2. What are the primary feelings expressed by the writer?

3. What do you think the others did to the writer? Why do you think they treated her the way they did?

4. Is the writer's worth as a person related to the way she was treated by others? If so, how?

Gain with Goals

Developmental Perspective

Although adolescents at this stage still prefer to live in the present, they are reaching an age where it is important to begin setting goals. Having realistic goals can have a positive effect on time management and academic achievement.

Objectives

▷ To differentiate between short-term and long-term goals

▷ To distinguish between realistic and unrealistic goals

▷ To learn how to establish short-term and long-term goals

Materials

▷ A copy of the Gain with Goals–Worksheet (Handout 15) for each student

▷ Pencil and paper for each student

▷ A sheet of newsprint, a marker, and a roll of masking tape for each group of four students

Procedure

1. Introduce the lesson by asking students to define the word *goal* (plan, purpose, or object of effort or ambition). Next, ask them to explain the difference between short- and long-term goals (short-term goals are more immediate and usually lead up to a long-term goal, which is in the future). Give an example: A long-term goal might be to get into a state university; a short-term goal would be to study for tests in order to do well in courses and keep a good grade point average. Ask students to raise their hands if they do the following:

   ► Routinely set short-term goals

   ► Routinely set long-term goals

   ► Routinely follow through on the goals they set

   ► Think they benefit from setting goals

2. Distribute the Gain with Goals–Worksheet (Handout 15) to each student. Invite students to work with partners to identify their responses. When students have responded to the worksheet, discuss their answers in the total group, emphasizing the difference between realistic and unrealistic goals in terms of attainability.

3. Ask students to form groups of four. Distribute a sheet of newsprint, a marker, and a roll of masking tape to each group. Assign each group one of the following topics:

   ► Summer plans

   ► Making money

   ► Making friends

> ▶ Achieving in school
>
> ▶ Achieving in sports, theater, or music
>
> ▶ Getting a job

Ask each group first to brainstorm how to set short-term and long-term goals: What factors do they need to consider? Next, have them clarify the distinction between realistic and unrealistic goals. On the basis of this discussion, ask each group to write two examples of realistic short-term goals and two examples of realistic long-term goals relative to the assigned topic.

4. Allow time for each group to share their examples with the total group. As they share, clarify as necessary the distinctions between long- and short-term goals and realistic and unrealistic goals.

5. Ask each student to choose a personal example and write at least one short-term and one long-term goal. Invite sharing.

6. Discuss the Content and Personalization Questions.

Discussion

CONTENT QUESTIONS

1. How can you tell whether a goal is realistic?

2. What do you see as the major difference between short-term and long-term goals?

3. Do you think it is important to set goals? Why or why not?

4. What do you think prevents people from setting goals?

5. What do you think prevents people from achieving goals?

PERSONALIZATION QUESTIONS

1. Do you usually set short-term goals? If so, do you usually achieve them? If not, what gets in the way?

2. Do you usually set long-term goals? If so, do you usually achieve them? If not, what gets in the way?

3. Can you think of an example from your own life when you did set a goal and it paid off?

4. Can you think of a time when you didn't set a goal but wish you had? How might the outcome have been different if you had set a goal?

5. How can you apply what you have learned from this lesson to your goal-setting behavior?

Follow-up Activity

Ask each student to set an achievable goal for the week. At the end of the week, have students check with partners to share their progress and revise their goals as necessary.

Gain with Goals

WORKSHEET

Name: _____ Date: _____

Instructions: Read the following goals. Circle R for realistic goals and U for unrealistic goals. Circle ST for short-term goals and LT for long-term goals.

R   **U**   1. Getting ready to go jogging for the first time, you set your goal for three miles.

R   **U**   2. You got 75 out of 100 points on your last Spanish test. Your goal for the next test is to get 80 out of 100 points.

R   **U**   3. You are a sophomore in high school. Your goal is to be a famous actress by the time you are 20.

R   **U**   4. Your goal is to buy a car by the time you turn 16 next month. So far you have saved 100 dollars.

R   **U**   5. Your goal is to go out with three girls before the end of the school year. It is March, and you have gone out with two so far.

ST   **LT**   1. Your goal is to move up from second-chair to first-chair saxophone in the high school band.

ST   **LT**   2. Your goal is to be rich.

ST   **LT**   3. Your goal is to own a car that runs.

ST   **LT**   4. Your goal is to get married and live in the suburbs.

ST   **LT**   5. Your goal is to pass algebra.

Make a Decision

Developmental Perspective

Although their reasoning abilities are improving, adolescents at this stage of development are still more logical at some times than at others. Most have the capacity to see alternatives, but they often lack the experience and self-understanding to make appropriate choices. Because they increasingly face more difficult decisions, they need to work continually on refining their skills in this area.

Objective

▷ To learn a specific decision-making process

Materials

▷ A copy of the Make a Decision–Worksheet (Handout 16) and the Make a Decision–Model (Handout 17) for each student

▷ Pencil and paper for each student

Procedure

1. Introduce the lesson by sharing the idea that decision making is a process in which a person chooses from one or more alternatives. Indicate that unless there is more than one course of action, a decision is not required.

2. Distribute the Make a Decision–Worksheet (Handout 16) to each student. Have students complete the worksheet. Then discuss their responses, and encourage conversation about the factors in decision making.

3. Distribute the Make a Decision–Model (Handout 17) to each student. Discuss the steps involved in decision making. Then ask each student to think of a decision he or she needs to make. Have students work through the steps by writing their responses in the blanks on the handout.

4. Invite students to find partners and share the steps in the model as applied to personal decisions.

5. Discuss the Content and Personalization Questions.

Discussion

CONTENT QUESTIONS

1. Which of the true/false questions were the most challenging for you to answer?

2. Which of the questions were the easiest to answer?

3. What is your opinion of the steps in the decision-making model?

PERSONALIZATION QUESTIONS

1. When you make a decision, do you follow the steps outlined in the model? If you do, how do you think this affects your decisions? If you don't, what effect do you think the model would have on your decisions if you used it?

2. How do you feel about your ability to make decisions? Do you feel the same way about your ability to make both simple decisions and more difficult ones?

Follow-up Activity

Ask students to apply the decision-making model to decisions they have to make. Allow time for them to report back on the process.

Make a Decision

WORKSHEET

Name: _____ Date: _____

Instructions: Read the following statements about decision making, and circle T (true) or F (false) for each statement.

T F   1. Decisions are limited by what you are capable of doing.

T F   2. Decisions are determined by what is available in your environment.

T F   3. Decisions are limited by what you are willing to do.

T F   4. To make good decisions, you need to know your values, your abilities, and something about yourself.

T F   5. There are some decisions over which you have little control.

T F   6. Some decisions are more important than others.

T F   7. Some decisions are automatic, habitual.

T F   8. People have direct control over decisions but not over outcomes.

T F   9. Decisions are based on what you want and what you know.

T F   10. Good decision making has nothing to do with a favorable outcome.

T F   11. You have to make most decisions without consulting others.

T F   12. Making a good decision requires luck.

Make a Decision

MODEL

Name: _____ Date: _____

Work through the decision-making model using a decision you need to make.

1. What decision do you need to make? _____

2. What do you want? _____

   _____

3. What are the possible alternatives? _____

   _____

   _____

   _____

4. What are the risks and/or benefits associated with each alternative? _____

   _____

   _____

   _____

5. What information do you need in order to make an informed decision? _____

   _____

   _____

6. Where (or from whom) can you obtain this information? _____

   _____

   _____

7. What is your decision? _____

   _____

Weigh the Risks

Developmental Perspective

Although they are continuing to develop abstract thinking skills, many adolescents at this stage still lack the ability to make sound decisions consistently. Because they still see themselves as invulnerable, they may ignore risks or not even consider risks because of the inconsistency in their logical thinking. Ignoring risks can have serious negative consequences.

Objective

▷ To identify risks associated with decision making

Materials

▷ A copy of the Weigh the Risks–Worksheet (Handout 18) and a pencil for each student

Procedure

1. Read the following narrative to students, and ask them to think about the risks involved in the decision Ricardo made:

   Ricardo was 15 years old and didn't have a driver's license, nor had he taken driver's education. Nevertheless, without his dad's permission, he frequently took the car and drove around town. So far his dad hadn't caught on, and Ricardo hadn't ever been stopped by the cops. One night his dad wasn't home, and Ricardo didn't have access to a car. He really wanted to go out to the country to a party, but he couldn't find anybody who could give him a ride. Then he had an idea. Because he mowed the neighbors' lawn, he had a key to their garage. He knew that Bud kept the key to his car in the ignition and that his bedroom was on the opposite side of the house from the garage. Ricardo thought he could easily get the car out of the garage without Bud's hearing a thing. So after the lights had been out for a while, Ricardo went over to Bud's house and borrowed the car.

2. Discuss the possible risks involved in Ricardo's decision. Then have students assess the degree of each risk, using a continuum of 1 (low risk) to 5 (high risk). Elicit discussion about the way students weighed the risks.

3. Distribute the Weigh the Risks–Worksheet (Handout 18) to each student. Ask students to work in pairs to complete the worksheet. When they have finished, have each pair discuss their responses with another pair.

4. Discuss the Content and Personalization Questions.

Discussion

CONTENT QUESTIONS

1. What factors did you have to consider in identifying risks?
2. Were there some situations in which you didn't think there were any risks? (Invite sharing.)
3. Which situations did you feel had the most risks associated with them?

PERSONALIZATION QUESTIONS

1. When you make a decision, do you always weigh the risks? If so, has this been helpful for you?
2. If you don't weigh the risks, what stops you from doing this? Is there a risk involved in ignoring the risks?
3. Some teenagers weigh the risks but feel they can beat the odds. Have you or others you know done this? If so, what were the results? Do you think this is a smart thing to do?

Follow-up Activity

Ask each student to interview two older students about weighing the risks when they make decisions and how they think doing so affects their decision-making ability. Allow time for students to discuss their findings with the total group.

Weigh the Risks

WORKSHEET–PAGE 1

Names: _____ Date: _____

Instructions: Read each situation. For each one, identify the possible risks, and circle the number indicating what you think is the degree of risk.

1. You have a test to study for, but you have an *A* going in the course, so you decide to go to the mall instead.

   Possible risks   **Degree of risk**

   _____   Low   1   2   3   4   5   High

   _____   Low   1   2   3   4   5   High

2. You don't want your parents to know you are meeting your boyfriend (or girlfriend) at the bowling alley, so you have a friend pick you up, and you tell your parents you are going to a movie.

   Possible risks   **Degree of risk**

   _____   Low   1   2   3   4   5   High

   _____   Low   1   2   3   4   5   High

3. Your mother usually waits up for you to come home. Tonight you had too much to drink and are a little past your curfew.

   Possible risks   **Degree of risk**

   _____   Low   1   2   3   4   5   High

   _____   Low   1   2   3   4   5   High

4. You like a girl (or guy) that your parents warned you not to have anything to do with. You are still continuing to see her (or him) at school, which is also the school your brother attends.

   Possible risks   **Degree of risk**

   _____   Low   1   2   3   4   5   High

   _____   Low   1   2   3   4   5   High

Weigh the Risks

WORKSHEET–PAGE 2

5. A kid offers to sell you a hit of acid, and you buy it.

    Possible risks   **Degree of risk**

    _____   Low 1 2 3 4 5 High

    _____   Low 1 2 3 4 5 High

6. You think your curfew is unreasonable, so you
    come in at 2:00 A.M. instead of midnight.

    Possible risks   **Degree of risk**

    _____   Low 1 2 3 4 5 High

    _____   Low 1 2 3 4 5 High

7. You and your boyfriend had sex and didn't
    use protection.

    Possible risks   **Degree of risk**

    _____   Low 1 2 3 4 5 High

    _____   Low 1 2 3 4 5 High

8. You have been very depressed, and you decide
    to take a bunch of pills to ease your pain.

    Possible risks   **Degree of risk**

    _____   Low 1 2 3 4 5 High

    _____   Low 1 2 3 4 5 High

9. Write your own: _____

    _____

    Possible risks   **Degree of risk**

    _____   Low 1 2 3 4 5 High

    _____   Low 1 2 3 4 5 High

Dangerous Decisions

Developmental Perspective

Whether they want to try things they have never tried, they want to see if they can get by with something, or they simply don't think things through carefully, adolescents may make decisions that have dangerous outcomes. Helping them learn to anticipate outcomes is critical at this stage of development.

Objective

▷ To learn to assess the consequences of decisions

Materials

▷ A copy of the Dangerous Decisions–Story (Handout 19) for each student

Procedure

1. Introduce the lesson by asking students to think of examples of what they would consider dangerous decisions. Invite discussion of examples and ask why students would classify them as dangerous.

2. Distribute the Dangerous Decisions–Story (Handout 19) to each student. Ask students to read the story. When they have finished, have them form groups of four and discuss whether or not they think the decision in the story was a dangerous one, what the consequences were or could be, and how this decision compares with examples of dangerous decisions shared in the earlier discussion.

3. Discuss the Content and Personalization Questions.

Discussion

CONTENT QUESTIONS

1. What distinguishes a dangerous decision from one that isn't?

2. Do you think teenagers consider the dangers of decisions before making them? If not, what stops them from thinking about the consequences? Do you think it would be better if they did?

3. Do you think teenagers make dangerous decisions to see if they can get away with something or to see what something is like? In addition to these reasons, what else do you think motivates teenagers to make decisions that could be dangerous?

PERSONALIZATION QUESTIONS

1. Have you ever made a decision you would consider dangerous? If so, how do you feel about it in retrospect?

2. As a general rule, do you think most of the decisions you make could be classified as dangerous? If so, have your decisions had negative consequences?

3. Is there anything you would like to change about your decision-making behavior? If so, how will you do this?

Follow-up Activity

Ask each student to reflect on past decisions and write about a decision he or she made that was or could have been dangerous. Students who have never made dangerous decisions can write about hypothetical decisions they would consider dangerous.

Dangerous Decisions

STORY—PAGE 1

For months I've been messing around with drugs . . . mostly pot and alcohol. I didn't think it was any big deal since all of my friends were doing it. After what happened about a month ago, I swore I wasn't going to drink again; I got so sick. I was at a keg party. I hadn't even wanted to go, but I'd already paid for it, so I thought I'd better get my money's worth. I knew when I went that I would get drunk quick and then start sobering up so when I went home my parents wouldn't know I'd been drinking. Well, for some reason I just kept drinking, and I was still really drunk when I got home. Luckily, my parents were in bed. I felt so awful, and my hangover lasted all the next day.

After that experience, I told my boyfriend, Jerod, that I didn't want him to let me get that drunk again. He agreed, and the next weekend all we did was smoke a little pot—no big deal. Things were like that for a while, but then they got out of hand. Jerod dropped out of school because his grades were so bad. He got a job. Because he was working, he had a lot more money, so he started buying more pot and crank. Pretty soon both of us were back to using a lot more. He was stoned or high most of the time, but then he lost his job, so he started dealing. I was beginning to get upset with him and told him I didn't want to go out with him if he was going to throw his life away. I at least had some goals for myself, and even though I really liked him, I couldn't see myself with a loser. So for a while I didn't have much to do with him, but I really didn't have all that many friends, so I started hanging out at his house again. One day I was at school, and a kid offered to sell me a hit of acid. I told him I didn't have any money, which was the truth. There was part of me that wanted to try it; I just wondered what it would be like. But I didn't have the money, so I told him no. Then later that day a kid who owed me money paid me back. I knew it wasn't enough to buy the acid, so I just forgot about it. But as I was leaving school, the kid approached me again and asked if I'd want to buy the acid the next day. I told him that I'd just gotten some money and he said he'd sell it to me for 7 dollars. I bought it.

Dangerous Decisions

STORY—PAGE 2

I went over to Jerod's house and that's when the nightmare started. I had a horrible trip. I was so freaked out. Everything was distorted, and I just couldn't come out of it. I was scared of everybody in the room, and it seemed like I was in an echo chamber at times. I felt totally disconnected from everything, I was off in my own world, and I sort of knew what was happening but in other ways I didn't. It got so bad I just wanted to die. My mind was just racing and I couldn't get it to stop. Everything was in slow motion. Jerod got really scared because he'd never seen anyone have such a bad trip. He called his dad, and his dad said Jerod should take me to a hospital. But we didn't want my parents to know, so he just kept trying to be there for me. It was horrible. Finally after about eight hours I was a little better, and he had to take me home. I didn't know what I was going to do. My parents were in bed, so I just went to my room and locked myself in. Jerod called me and we just kept talking most of the night so I wouldn't be scared and so he would know I was all right. I was a little better the next day, but it took me so long to come off it. No one I had ever known had had a trip that bad.

Now I'm worried. I used to blame my drinking and drugs on my boyfriend because I could always get it from him. But I bought this acid all by myself, and I know I can get it again. I don't want to do it again, but there is still part of me that just wants to see if it wouldn't be so bad the second time. I know I had some really bad stuff, and maybe if it was better, I would like it. Other kids trip in school, and they don't experience anything like I did. But on the other hand, I can't imagine why I'd want to put myself in that situation again and risk going through what I did. I'm upset with myself for doing it. I'm just afraid I'll do it again. I have never been so scared in my life. It's like I know what I should do, but I just don't know if I can do it.

—Heather, Age 16

the **PASSPORT** PROGRAM

GRADE
11

Self-Development
ACTIVITY
1   Who I Am: Inside and Outside
2   Down on Myself, Up on Myself
3   Self-Respect
4   Becoming Independent

Emotional Development
ACTIVITY
1   Help Yourself to Happiness
2   Let Go of It
3   Crying on the Inside
4   De-Stressing Stress

Social Development
ACTIVITY
1   I Need You
2   I Wish They Were Different
3   Dating "Do's" and "Don'ts"
4   Romantic Relationships

Cognitive Development
ACTIVITY
1   Predict the Outcome
2   Make a Plan
3   Rational Thinking
4   Evaluating Decisions

Who I Am: Inside & Outside

Developmental Perspective

Along with achieving independence, preoccupation with one's identity is a primary task at this stage of development. It is important for adolescents to try on various ways of thinking, feeling, and behaving in order to find out more about themselves. Part of this process is recognizing the parts they keep hidden from others.

Objectives

▷ To learn more about who one is becoming in one's identity quest

▷ To learn how to accept oneself

Materials

▷ A small lunch-size paper bag, a marker, a pencil, a sheet of paper, and a pair of scissors for each student

▷ A large paper bag with the following phrases written on the outside: *no sense of humor, fun to be with occasionally, below average student, lousy musician*

▷ Individual slips of paper (to be put inside the bag), with the following words or phrases written on them: *insecure, impatient, unattractive, occasionally rebellious*

Procedure

1. Introduce the lesson by reviewing the concepts outlined in the Developmental Perspective.

2. Distribute a set of supplies to each student. Ask students to think about how they "look" on the outside . . . the images they project to others. Encourage them to think beyond physical characteristics. Ask students to write words or draw symbols representing these characteristics on the outsides of their bags. Then, have them think about who they are on the inside . . . the feelings, problems, issues, high/low points, or personality characteristics that they keep hidden from others. Have them write these on their sheets of paper and cut the paper into slips so that each item is on a separate slip. They should put these slips inside their bags.

3. Invite students to find partners and share the outsides of the bags and as much of the contents as they feel comfortable sharing.

4. Display the large paper bag and read the words on the outside of the bag. Then read the words on the slips inside the bag. Ask students whether they consider the descriptors basically positive or negative. Engage them in a discussion about whether a teenager who perceives him- or herself as having basically negative qualities is a worthless individual. Stress that all people are worthwhile regardless of their abilities or their actions. That is not to say that people can't work to improve things they can change, but even if they didn't, they would still be worthwhile. Elicit students' reactions to this concept.

5. Discuss the Content and Personalization Questions

Discussion

CONTENT QUESTIONS

1. Was it more difficult to think about things to put on the outside or the inside of the bag?

2. What do you think it is about the things on the inside that people want to protect, as opposed to being open about them?

PERSONALIZATION QUESTIONS

1. Are there some people who have access to all or some of the things you put inside the bag? What is it about those people that allows you to feel comfortable sharing these things with them?

2. Which are you more comfortable with, the inside you or the outside you?

3. Do you think some of the things on the inside will ever be on the outside? (Invite discussion.)

4. Even if you have some things you consider negative on the outside or the inside of your bag, does that make you a worthless person?

Follow-up Activity

Encourage students to keep their bags and add to the outside or the inside as they continue to discover more about themselves.

Down on Myself, Up on Myself

Developmental Perspective

Although many adolescents are by this stage more self-assured and no longer feel the need to be carbon copies of their peers, others continue to struggle with self-acceptance. Despite their more advanced thinking skills, it is not at all uncommon for adolescents to think very dichotomously and judge themselves as good or bad, as opposed to seeing themselves as complex individuals with positive and negative characteristics. As a result, it is very easy for adolescents to get down on themselves, and this can lead to other problems.

Objectives

▷ To identify ways one puts oneself down

▷ To identify one's positive qualities

Materials

▷ A sponge and a pan of water

▷ A copy of the Down on Myself, Up on Myself–Worksheet (Handout 1) for each student

▷ Pencil and paper for each student

▷ A sheet of newsprint listing the following discussion questions:

Why do some adolescents get so down on themselves?

Just because some adolescents make some mistakes, should they consider themselves total failures?

Once they get down on themselves, how can they turn this around? How can they start to feel better about themselves?

Procedure

1. Introduce the lesson by asking for a volunteer to pick up the sponge. Ask the volunteer to describe what the sponge feels like. Then have him or her place the sponge in the pan of water and lift it out without squeezing it dry. Ask the volunteer to describe how the sponge feels after it has been in the water (heavier). Use this analogy as a way of introducing the topic for this lesson. Explain that it is often easy for adolescents to get down on themselves, and once this happens they tend to soak up the negative and not let in any of the positive. They may interpret others' feedback or behavior only from a negative perspective, or they may discount positives because they feel so down on themselves. Invite students to share opinions about this.

2. Distribute the Down on Myself, Up on Myself–Worksheet (Handout 1) to each student. Ask students to read and respond to the worksheet. Stress that their responses will not be shared with others.

3. Have students form groups of five, and have each group appoint a recorder. Then display the newsprint with the discussion questions, and ask the small groups to address these questions.

4. Have students make lists of several positive characteristics they possess. Ask them to write themselves short letters telling how they can stop being sponges that soak up the negative. (If they are not down on themselves, have them write about how they might help friends who are.)

5. Discuss the Content and Personalization Questions.

Discussion

CONTENT QUESTIONS

1. Why do you think some teenagers get so down on themselves?

2. Do you think that just because some teenagers make mistakes, they should consider themselves total failures?

3. Do you think it is possible for teenagers who are down on themselves to start seeing themselves in a more positive light? If so, how can they do this?

PERSONALIZATION QUESTIONS

1. Do you tend to get down on yourself?

2. Can you forgive yourself if you make a mistake? If so, how do you do this?

3. Can you identify your positive qualities, or do your negative ones overshadow them? If they do, what do you think you can do to change this?

Follow-up Activity

Ask students to monitor their negative thoughts about themselves. Have them put the negative thoughts in writing and try to substitute something positive for each negative thought.

Down on Myself, Up on Myself

WORKSHEET

Name: _____ Date: _____

Instructions: Read the following actual quotes from teenagers. Circle any that apply to you, or add your own. If you don't get down on yourself, don't circle anything. No one else will see your responses.

1. I am so used to putting myself down that I can't think of any strengths.

2. I never feel like I'm good enough.

3. I'm not worth living with; I've put everybody through too much.

4. My big, fat, ugly, screwed-up body should just disappear.

5. Everyone hates me; I can't name one person who doesn't.

6. I'm a loser. All I ever do is make mistakes.

7. Some kids can just sit there and be perfectly normal. I don't see myself as normal.

8. I have finally figured out that I feel like a nobody.

9. People can tell me they love me, but I really feel they hate me. Why would they love me?

10. I can't stand looking at myself in the mirror. I hate what I see.

11. Why am I so ugly, stupid, shy, and weird?

12. I don't know why my parents worry about me. I'm not worth worrying about.

Self-Respect

Developmental Perspective

Although most adolescents at this stage of development are becoming more self-assured than they were in early adolescence, there are nevertheless many who don't have very good self-concepts or who compromise themselves in order to be accepted by peers. As a result, they may act in ways that demonstrate lack of self-respect.

Objectives

▷ To differentiate between self-respect and disrespect

▷ To identify ways to change things one doesn't respect in oneself but to accept oneself as worthwhile regardless of these things

Materials

▷ A chalkboard

▷ A copy of the Self-Respect–Stories (Handout 2), paper, and a pencil for each student

Procedure

1. Introduce the lesson by asking students to define the term *respect* (to hold in high regard). Discuss the difference between self-respect and disrespect for self. Encourage students to generate examples of indicators of self-respect relative to the way they think, feel, and behave. Have them do the same for disrespect. List the examples on the board.

2. Distribute a copy of the Self-Respect–Stories (Handout 2) to each student. Ask students to read these stories and answer the questions, on a separate sheet of paper, if necessary. When they have finished, break them into triads to discuss their reactions to the stories and their responses to the questions.

3. Discuss the Content and Personalization Questions.

Discussion

CONTENT QUESTIONS

1. In what ways did Maria demonstrate self-respect? In what ways did she demonstrate disrespect for herself?

2. In what ways did Chad demonstrate self-respect? In what ways did he demonstrate disrespect for himself?

3. What do you think kept the teenagers in the stories "stuck" in behaviors they disrespected in themselves?

4. Does the fact that Maria and Chad did some things that caused them to lose respect for themselves mean that they are not worthy of respect at all?

PERSONALIZATION QUESTIONS

1. Have you ever been in a situation in which you have experienced disrespect for yourself? If so, what feelings did you have about this?

2. Is it possible to change your attitudes or behaviors so you don't disrespect yourself? (Invite discussion.)

3. Even if there are some things you disrespect about yourself, does that mean you are a worthless individual?

Follow-up Activity

Have students write short papers on ways they do or can demonstrate self-respect. Invite them to share their papers with a partner.

Self-Respect

STORIES–PAGE 1

Name: _____ Date: _____

Instructions: Read these two stories. Answer the questions at the end of each story.

Maria's Story

I was 16 when I first met Jason. He had just moved into my school district. At first things were great. I was a cheerleader, and he was captain of the football team. After football season he started using pot–not a lot, and mostly on weekends. After a while, though, he got into crank and was smoking pot more regularly. He was always high when we went out, and I didn't like it at all. But if I said anything about it he'd get mean, so I just kept quiet.

By the time school started the next fall, Jason had no intention of going back to school. He was using drugs a lot and had to work to support his habit. I was angry and finally started to confront him. My parents and stepmother were always trying to convince me that I should stop dating him. They knew he was never very nice to me, and they couldn't understand how I could do this to myself. They were also concerned that I would start using drugs. I knew that this would never happen, but it got to the point where I was fighting with them all the time because they tried to prevent me from going out with him or kept nagging me about his drug abuse.

My relationship with Jason also affected my relationships with some of my friends. They would see how upset I'd get when he was mean to me, and several times they heard him call me every name in the book and slap me around. I was ashamed. They kept asking me why I'd keep going with someone who treated me that way. I knew the reason I did was because I kept hoping he'd get off drugs and change. Then I knew he'd treat me better. I knew he could be nice, so I just kept hoping that time would come again. And sometimes it did, but I never knew when. More often than not, though, he'd yell at me, not show up when we were supposed to go out, or slap me around. I had to hide that from my parents and my friends, but one night it got so bad I couldn't. We were driving around in the country, and I told him I couldn't go on like this. He went berserk. He started hitting me. I got out of the car and started to run. He came after me, but luckily another car came by and picked me up. After that my parents got an injunction against him so he wouldn't come near me.

Self-Respect

STORIES—PAGE 2

It's embarrassing. I still really care about him a lot, but none of my friends can understand why I'd stay in a relationship where I got treated like that. Now I can't see him, and I know I should just forget about him. I don't feel good about myself for allowing him to treat me like that.

–Maria, Age 16

1. What are some ways Maria showed respect for herself?

2. In what ways did she demonstrate disrespect for herself?

3. Why do you think Maria allowed herself to be controlled by Jason? How did this affect her self-respect?

Chad's Story

I had been going with Nicole for about two months. She said she really cared about me, and I liked her a lot, too. At first everything was great. We never fought or argued except when we were joking around. Everyone considered us the "perfect couple." It got to the point where I would do anything for her. Before I met her, I drank a lot and did drugs, but after we started going out, I cut way back on that. Things were great for a while, but then it seemed like whenever I would call, she'd either not be there and never return my calls, or she'd have some excuse for not going out. One night she told me she had to study for a test, but later I saw her car parked in front of the bowling alley. The next day at school I asked her about it, and she said her sister had taken her car. I wanted to believe her, so I dropped the subject.

I asked her out for Saturday night. She said fine, but just before I went to pick her up, she called and said she had the flu and couldn't go out. I asked her if she still wanted to go with me and she said she did, so I told her to call me when she felt better. I went out with some of my friends and called Nicole later to see how she was feeling. There was no answer. I kept telling myself that maybe she was just sleeping and didn't hear the phone, but the next day one of my friends told me he had seen her cruising with a guy from another school. I called her the next day and told her what my friend had said. She denied it. I told her I thought she was lying, and she got mad and said I had

Self-Respect

STORIES–PAGE 3

no right to call her a liar. I didn't want to lose her, so I apologized and bought her flowers, and we made up. Things were pretty good for about a month. Then she broke up with me over some stupid reason, and I was a mess. I told all my friends to leave me alone, and all I did for two weeks was drink to try and kill the pain.

But then she called, and we made up. But it started all over again. This time she was very controlling. If I went out and didn't call her, she was furious. I started feeling trapped. I couldn't figure out how to please her; first she wanted her freedom, and then she wanted me with her all the time. I couldn't win. We fought all the time, and she called me some very ugly things. I tried not to get that way with her, but it didn't change the way she acted. One night we had agreed to go to a movie, just the two of us, but when I went to pick her up, her stepmother said she'd gone to a party. I drove around and found her, which made her furious. In front of a whole bunch of people she just went off on me, swearing at me and yelling. I finally just left, but when I was riding around I saw her get out of another guy's car. She called me the next day and lied about it.

I told Nicole I was tired of being treated like this and I wanted out of the relationship. She promised to change, but I finally had enough courage to tell her I wasn't waiting around. She had lied to me, humiliated me in front of my friends, and gone out with other guys behind my back. I was beginning to think that there was something wrong with me and that no one wanted to be with me. My friends kept saying that wasn't true but that I wouldn't be able to see it unless I got out of the relationship. I guess I finally had to tell myself that enough was enough.

–Chad, Age 17

1. What are some ways Chad showed respect for himself?

2. In what ways did he demonstrate disrespect for himself?

3. Why do you think Chad allowed himself to be controlled by Nicole? How did this affect his self-respect?

Becoming Independent

Developmental Perspective

One of the fundamental tasks at this stage of development is becoming independent. Although this is something most adolescents claim to want more than anything, at the same time there may be anxiety associated with becoming emotionally and economically independent of parents.

Objectives

▷ To identify what it means to be independent, ways one is independent, and feelings associated with independence

▷ To identify what it means to be dependent, ways one is dependent, and feelings associated with dependence

Materials

▷ A chalkboard

▷ Paper and pencil for each student

Procedure

1. Introduce the lesson by writing the word *independent* on the board and asking students to share ideas about what being independent means to them. Then write the word *dependent* and elicit ideas about what this means. Explain to students that at this stage of development, they may already be independent in many ways or at least want to be. However, most of them are probably still dependent as well. Elicit some discussion about who or what they are trying to become independent from and how they are attempting to do so.

2. Have students take out paper and pencil and respond to the following items:

   ► Ways I am already independent and how I feel about that

   ► Ways I am still dependent and how I feel about that

   ► Ways I would like to—or think I should be—more independent and how I feel about that

3. In small groups, have students share their responses to the three items. Following their discussion, ask them to share examples and feelings with the total group.

4. Discuss the Content and Personalization Questions.

Discussion

CONTENT QUESTIONS

1. What feelings did you identify for ways in which you are already independent? Do you consider these positive, negative, or neutral?

2. What feelings did you identify for ways in which you are still dependent? Do you consider these positive, negative, or neutral?

3. What feelings did you identify for ways in which you would like to become more independent?

4. Do you think it is normal to experience some anxiety about becoming more independent, especially as you think about leaving home after high school? If you do experience anxiety, what are some approaches you have found effective for dealing with it? (Explain that since anxiety is almost always about a future event, it is easy to imagine the worst or think that there will be no one to rely on if a problem arises. For example, teenagers may be anxious about taking care of themselves if they get sick once they move away from home and are living independently. They may forget that they can still ask for help from others if they need it.)

5. If a person is independent, do you think he or she will also sometimes be dependent? (Ask students for examples.)

6. Do you think becoming more independent means that you will also have more responsibilities? If so, how do you feel about this? (Ask students for examples.)

PERSONALIZATION QUESTIONS

1. At this point in your life, do you see yourself as more dependent or independent? How do you feel about this?

2. When you think about becoming more independent, what are you looking forward to about this independence? Is there anything about it that worries you? (Invite sharing.)

Follow-up Activity

Have students interview young people who are a year or two older to find out how they handle their independence and what new responsibilities they have as a result of being more independent.

Help Yourself to Happiness

Developmental Perspective

Although being overwhelmed by negative or ambivalent emotions is typical during adolescence, it is important to help adolescents identify ways to help themselves feel happier because they often act impulsively and deal with negative feelings in unhealthy ways. Helping them understand that feelings don't just happen–and that their attitudes and beliefs can influence the degree to which they experience happiness–gives them some emotional "tools."

Objectives

▷ To recognize the connection between thoughts and feelings

▷ To identify ways to change negative feelings to positive feelings

Materials

▷ A chalkboard

▷ A copy of the Help Yourself to Happiness–Information Sheet (Handout 3) for each student

▷ A sheet of newsprint and a marker for each group of four students

Procedure

1. Introduce the lesson with a brief discussion about the fact that during adolescence, negative emotions often seem more predominant than positive ones. Emphasize that since many negative emotions seem painful and overwhelming, it is easy to think they will never end or to deal with them in unhealthy or self-defeating ways. Invite students to react to these concepts. Explain that the purpose of this lesson is to help them identify ways to "help themselves to happiness."

2. Write the following statement on the board: "A happy person is a person with a certain set of attitudes, not a certain set of circumstances."

3. Divide students into groups of four. Have them discuss what this statement means and whether they agree or disagree with it. After several minutes of discussion, invite sharing of reactions with the total group.

4. Distribute a sheet of newsprint and a marker to each group, along with a Help Yourself to Happiness–Information Sheet (Handout 3) for each student. Have students read the handout and, as a group, react to what they read. Ask them to generate their own quotations reflecting their thoughts about what happiness is and how one finds it. Have each group write their quotations on the newsprint. Invite each group to share their quotations, and post the newsprint sheets in the room for future reference.

5. Discuss the Content and Personalization Questions.

Discussion

CONTENT QUESTIONS

1. Did you agree with the first quotation about happiness? Why or why not?
2. When you read the Help Yourself to Happiness–Information Sheet, what ideas did you agree with? What did you disagree with?
3. How can changing the way you think help you be happier?

PERSONALIZATION QUESTIONS

1. Do you think you can "help yourself to happiness"? Have you ever done this? (Invite sharing of examples.)
2. Can you apply the quote "A happy person is a person with a certain set of attitudes, not a certain set of circumstances" to your life? If so, how?
3. Have your ideas about how to feel happy changed as a result of this activity? If so, in what ways?

Follow-up Activity

Invite students to make posters or bumper stickers reflecting their attitudes and beliefs about happiness.

Help Yourself to Happiness

INFORMATION SHEET

Lots of people mistakenly think that their feelings just happen–that events occur and they automatically feel certain ways about them. However, consider the fact that the same event could happen to two different people, and they each might have different feelings about it. For example, suppose both you and your friend had been asked to a dance. On the day of the dance there is a huge snowstorm, and the dance is canceled. You might feel devastated, and your friend might merely be disappointed. Why the difference? If you are a young woman, you might be thinking, "This is awful. I just spent all this money on a new dress, and now I can't wear it. I can't stand the thought of staying home and not seeing my boyfriend tonight. Why did this have to happen?" If you are a young man, you obviously wouldn't be upset about a new dress, but you might feel devastated about not getting to go out with your girlfriend or upset about the thought of being snowed in with your parents on a Friday night.

But what about your friend? He or she is disappointed, but not devastated. Your friend is probably thinking, "I don't like the thought of staying home, but I guess there's not much I can do about it since the weather is so bad. I was looking forward to having a lot of fun with my date. Oh, well, I guess we'll just have to wait until the dance is rescheduled."

Notice that the devastated female did what we call *awfulizing*. And when she did this, she forgot that the dance would be rescheduled and that she would eventually have the chance to wear her new dress. When people awfulize, they blow things out of proportion and make them seem much worse than they *really* are. This is what can lead to unhappiness.

If you want to "help yourself to happiness," you have to start thinking differently. You need to assess situations realistically: Are things really as catastrophic, awful, or terrible as you initially think, or are they bad but not horrible? Is it absolutely *impossible* to tolerate this, or would you just rather not? Another point to remember is not to blame yourself for everything; doing so only contributes to your unhappiness. For example, if you didn't have a date for the dance, don't automatically assume it's because you're stupid, ugly, or a klutz. Those things probably aren't true–and even if they were, it wouldn't mean you were a bad person.

The point is that happiness doesn't just happen. The way you think influences the degree to which you are happy or unhappy. If you challenge your thinking about a situation, you may not change unhappiness to elation, but you can feel less unhappy. The more you practice this type of thinking the better your chances that you won't feel as unhappy as much of the time.

Let Go of It

Developmental Perspective

Anger is a powerful emotion. Many young people seem to have difficulty letting go of their anger, in part because anger can be empowering, it can mask hurt, and it is familiar. However, anger stands in the way of effective problem solving and contributes to loss of control and impulsive behaviors that can have negative long-term effects.

Objective

▷ To learn how to let go of anger

Materials

▷ Paper and pencil for each student

▷ At least one newspaper and a pair of scissors for every four students

▷ Index cards, one per student

▷ For each student, an envelope containing five blank slips of paper

▷ Five balloons and five pieces of string for each student

Procedure

1. Introduce the lesson by asking for a show of hands from students who have trouble letting go of their anger. Discuss the reasons people hang on to anger, and stress the negative effects of anger described in the Developmental Perspective. Explain to students that the purpose of this lesson is to teach them how to let go of their anger.

2. Ask students to take out pencil and paper and quickly write down situations that they used to be angry about but no longer are. Engage them in a brief discussion of the reasons they are no longer angry about these situations. Indicate that people sometimes let go of anger because they can begin to put their problems in perspective by asking themselves, "In relation to other problems, how significant was this one?"

3. Have students form groups of four, and distribute the newspapers and scissors. Ask each group to go through the newspaper and cut out five articles they think depict problems that might provoke anger in the people involved (examples from Ann Landers' columns; factual articles about fighting, abuse, or disasters; and the like). Next, distribute the index cards, and have each student write an example of something that he or she is or has been angry about.

4. Within each group, ask students to imagine a continuum line on the floor in front of them. One end of the line represents the "very significant" category; the other end represents the "not very significant" category. Ask students to think about the problem articles they cut from the newspaper and try to situate them somewhere on the continuum. Then ask them to imagine where on the continuum they would put the problems they noted on the index cards.

5. Discuss the Content Questions. Then explain the following:

> Particularly with anger, it is sometimes so easy to get caught up in the emotion that we catastrophize about the problem, assume it will never go away, or hang on to the blame and the notion that things shouldn't be the way they are. Anger is often connected to the beliefs that it's not fair that this happened and that you can't stand that it did. One way to let go of the anger is to let go of the idea that everything in the world has to be fair. It would be nice if that were true, but in reality, it's not the way things always work. So letting go of anger sometimes means letting go of the ideas related to fairness and "shoulds."

6. Distribute the envelopes containing the slips of paper. Invite each student to think of five things he or she feels angry about and write them on the slips of paper. On the backs of the slips, ask students to write any reasons they think they should hold onto the anger. Then distribute the balloons and string. Ask students to think about what they wrote on the slips of paper and their reasons for holding on to the anger. If they are ready to let the anger go, they should put the slips inside the balloons (one per balloon). Stress the fact that there may be some things they are not ready to let go of yet, and they may decide to do so later. Conclude this part of the activity by having students blow the balloons up, tie the strings around them, and release them outside as a way of letting go of the anger. Then discuss the Personalization Questions.

Discussion

CONTENT QUESTIONS

1. Did you identify different problems at different points along the continuum?
2. Did considering problems in terms of a continuum help you put them in perspective?

PERSONALIZATION QUESTIONS

1. If you let go of some anger by releasing one or more balloons, what was it like for you to do this?
2. What did you need to do to be able to let go of the anger? Did you change your thinking? If so, in what way?

3. Is hanging onto your anger helpful for you in any way? If not, why do you think you continue to hold on to it?

4. Do you think the continuum technique might be useful to you for learning to put things in perspective and let go of your anger?

Follow-up Activity

Distribute several more balloons to each student, and invite students to identify other anger issues they would like to let go of using this procedure. Invite them to write journal entries about the effect this symbolic process has on their actual feelings.

Crying on the Inside

Developmental Perspective

Growing up can be a struggle, and for an adolescent, each experience becomes a lesson in living. Although adults may question why adolescents spend so much time alone in their rooms, this is how they process their experiences and think about who they are and how they feel. Sometimes adults have no idea of the degree to which this processing occurs because adolescents are adept at laughing on the outside and crying on the inside.

Objectives

▷ To distinguish between the image one projects to others and the feelings one keeps to oneself

▷ To identify the positive and the negative aspects of keeping some feelings inside

Materials

▷ A lunch-size paper bag, a felt-tipped pen, scissors, and a sheet of paper per student

▷ A sheet of newsprint with the following statement written on it:

> I feel like I'm leading a double life: first, the real me who is sad and depressed, and second, the fake me who acts like nothing is wrong. I can't explain my feelings to anyone because I don't even understand them myself. All I know is that I'm not the happy kid everyone seems to think I am.

Procedure

1. Introduce the activity by posting the sheet of newsprint with the statement.

2. Ask students to find partners and react to the statement, reflecting on its meaning and its relevance for young people at this stage in life. Invite sharing with the total group.

3. Distribute the paper bags and other materials. Ask each student to think about the image he or she projects to others on the outside and write words to describe this image on the outside of the paper bag. Then have students cut their sheets of paper into slips and on these slips, write words to describe who they are on the inside. Have them place the slips inside their bags. They can choose whether or not to share the bags' contents with others.

4. Have each student find a partner—someone he or she knows well. Invite partners to share the outsides of their bags. Invite them to give each other feedback on what they wrote. Encourage them to share the contents of the bags if they feel comfortable doing so.

5. Discuss the Content and Personalization Questions.

Discussion

CONTENT QUESTIONS

1. Was it more difficult to think of words for the outside or for the inside of the bag?

2. Why do you think people hide some of the things they really feel? Do you think this is good? Are there negative aspects of this?

PERSONALIZATION QUESTIONS

1. Were you able to identify with the statement on the newsprint? Why or why not?

2. Did you learn anything about yourself as you identified terms for the inside and the outside of your bag?

3. If you are a person who keeps feelings inside, why do you think you do this? What are the positive and negative aspects of this for you?

Follow-up Activity

Ask students to bring in songs that illustrate the "crying on the inside" theme. Provide time for them to share these in small groups.

De-Stressing Stress

Developmental Perspective

For a variety of reasons, life can be stressful for young people. Some become involved in so many activities that they have trouble managing their time to fit everything in, while others must work long hours to help support themselves. Still others experience the stress resulting from dysfunctional family situations or peer relationships. It is important to teach adolescents to identify and manage stress so they don't become overwhelmed and resort to unhealthy ways of coping.

Objectives

▷ To identify sources of stress

▷ To learn how to manage stress

Materials

▷ A copy of the De-Stressing Stress–Survey (Handout 4) and a pencil for each student

▷ A copy of the De-Stressing Stress–Solutions (Handout 5) for each student

Procedure

1. Introduce the activity with a discussion about stress. Explain that it is commonly referred to as "wear and tear on the body" and is an emotional condition that occurs when situations are overwhelming and coping methods are inadequate. Ask students if they can identify some of the common signs of stress (difficulty sleeping, irritability, excessive worrying, lack of patience, headaches or muscle tension, agitation or reckless behavior, difficulty getting along with others, change in eating habits). Ask for a show of hands indicating how many students have experienced stress.

2. Distribute the De-Stressing Stress–Survey (Handout 4) to each student. After students have completed the survey, have them share the results in triads.

3. After some discussion time, distribute the De-Stressing Stress–Solutions (Handout 5) to each student to read.

4. Discuss the Content and Personalization Questions.

Discussion

Content Questions

1. Look at the check marks in the "frequently" column on your survey. From the number of check marks, would you say you are or are not under a considerable amount of stress?

2. Is there any general pattern to the sources of your stress (for example, more stress at home, more at school, more with friends, and so on)?

3. Of the solutions given on the handout, which ones seem like they would help the most to reduce stress?

4. In addition to the solutions on the handout, can you think of others that might help to reduce stress?

Personalization Questions

1. If you had completed this survey a year ago, would you have responded to the items in the same way? If not, what has changed?

2. If your stress level is high, what do you think you can do to reduce it?

3. What did you learn from this lesson that might be helpful for you in managing your stress?

Follow-up Activity

Encourage each student to select one of the stress management solutions or identify a personal solution. Then, ask each student to target one area to work on and establish a contract with a partner. Partners can monitor each other to assess progress in stress reduction.

De-Stressing Stress

SURVEY

Name: _____ Date: _____

Instructions: Respond to each item by putting a check mark in the column that best describes how frequently you are stressed about that item.

	Frequently	Sometimes	Never
Parents	☐	☐	☐
Siblings	☐	☐	☐
Money	☐	☐	☐
Friendships	☐	☐	☐
Dating	☐	☐	☐
Sex	☐	☐	☐
The future	☐	☐	☐
Job	☐	☐	☐
Teachers	☐	☐	☐
School performance	☐	☐	☐
Extracurricular activities	☐	☐	☐
Rules at home or at school	☐	☐	☐
Expectations from others	☐	☐	☐
Expectations from self	☐	☐	☐
Expectations at school	☐	☐	☐
Being included or excluded	☐	☐	☐
Pressure to use drugs or alcohol	☐	☐	☐
Appearance	☐	☐	☐
Add your own:			
_____	☐	☐	☐
_____	☐	☐	☐
_____	☐	☐	☐

De-Stressing Stress

SOLUTIONS

1. When you begin to experience symptoms of stress, sit down and try to figure out what exactly is bothering you.

2. Next, tackle one problem or situation at a time. Write down everything about that situation that is stressful to you, and then check to see if you have all the facts. For example, if you get stressed out because your friend hasn't called you lately and you assume he or she doesn't like you anymore, find out what's really happening. Maybe your friend was grounded from the phone. Always check out your assumptions–you could be creating unnecessary stress for yourself by the way you think.

3. Try to distinguish immediate issues and stressors from those in the future. It is easy to become stressed out about things that may be months or even years away, and then you get overwhelmed because there is so much to do or think about. Separate out the issues that can be put on hold for a while. Mentally put them in a box, and put the box on the top shelf of the closet. Deal with those things after you have taken care of the more immediate concerns.

4. Don't forget to exercise. This helps reduce tension and is a proven stress reliever for many people. Also, be sure to eat regularly. Avoid junk food as much as possible!

5. Don't catastrophize over something that may not happen. In your mind, challenge yourself to find the evidence that something will or will not occur, and don't automatically assume the absolute worst. For example, don't get stressed out over a test, thinking that you will fail, that it will be the end of the world, and that it will certainly prove that you are stupid. First of all, if you did fail, it wouldn't be the end of the world . . . worse things could happen. Don't catastrophize over this one. And even if you did fail, it wouldn't make you a stupid person.

6. Do things that help you relax: Listen to music, read, or ask someone to give you a massage.

7. Make a stress management plan: Identify what you'd like to change, and then list several small steps you could take to make it happen. For example, if you don't like the way you look because you are overweight, agree to exercise every other day for 15 minutes, stop eating potato chips and candy bars, and drink only diet soda. Taking little steps isn't as overwhelming as taking big steps, and you are more likely to follow through.

8. Talk it out! Don't keep things bottled up inside because stress sometimes turns into anger. You might blow up and make matters worse.

I Need You

Developmental Perspective

Dependence in peer relationships is not at all uncommon at this age. Far too many young males and females think that they are nothing without their partners and that they can't exist without those relationships. As a result, they often stay in relationships far longer than they should and allow the partners to control their behavior, feelings, and thoughts. It is important for adolescents to understand the concept of unhealthy dependence so they don't continue to engage in these kinds of relationships as they move into adulthood.

Objective

▷ To distinguish between healthy and unhealthy dependence in relationships

Materials

▷ A chalkboard

▷ Paper and pencil for each student

▷ A copy of the I Need You–Codependence Characteristics (Handout 6) and the I Need You–Stories (Handout 7) for each student

Procedure

1. Discuss the meaning of the word *dependence* (relying on someone for support, being influenced or controlled) and how dependence can be healthy or unhealthy. Ask students for examples of healthy and unhealthy dependence, and list these on the board as they are identified. (For example, healthy dependence could be relying on a friend for support temporarily when something stressful or negative happens. Unhealthy dependence would be constantly needing the support and reassurance of others.) Introduce the term *codependence,* and distribute the I Need You–Codependence Characteristics (Handout 6) to each student. After students have read the handout, invite discussion about the concept.

2. Distribute the I Need You–Stories (Handout 7) to each student. Ask students to read these, keeping in mind the characteristics of codependence.

3. Have students form triads and discuss their reactions to the stories and their responses to the Content and Personalization Questions.

Discussion

CONTENT QUESTIONS

1. What do you see as the difference between healthy and unhealthy dependence?
2. What is your understanding of codependence? Do you think it is very common? Why do you think adolescents and adults become involved in these kinds of relationships?
3. How were the teenagers in these stories dependent and/or codependent?

PERSONALIZATION QUESTIONS

1. Have you been in a codependent relationship? If so, how did it affect you?
2. What is your definition of a healthy relationship? What steps can you take to make sure that you are in healthy relationships?

Follow-up Activity

Ask students to listen for songs that they think reflect unhealthy dependence and codependence. Invite them to share these with the group.

I Need You

CODEPENDENCE CHARACTERISTICS

When you are codependent, your good feelings about yourself
come from being liked by others.

When you are codependent, your attention is focused
on pleasing others.

When you are codependent, you feel better about yourself if
you can help other people solve their problems or fix their pain.

When you are codependent, you dress and act to please
other people.

When you are codependent, you put your own interests and
needs aside and spend time doing what others want to do.

When you are codependent, you are afraid of rejection,
and this influences what you say and do.

When you are codependent, you put aside your values to connect
with another person.

When you are codependent, you focus all your energy on
one person, and your social circle becomes smaller and smaller.

When you are codependent, your life revolves around
another person.

I Need You

STORIES–PAGE 1

Instructions: Think about the codependence characteristics as you read each of the stories.

Jill's Story

The past few months of my relationship with Ethan were long and no fun. It was like we both knew it should be over but we couldn't end it. I don't know why I had a hard time ending it, but I didn't feel the same without him. We broke up and got back together all the time. But when we weren't together, I felt like I needed to have him back again.

I always felt like he was my only friend and the only person I could talk to. I almost felt like I couldn't be happy without him. He always said things to make me think the reasons we broke up were all my fault. The funny thing is, most of the time it worked. I would blame myself and put myself down. I let him crush my emotions. I would then let him "make it all better" by saying that he was sorry and that he loved me.

I look back on it now, and I can't believe I was so gullible. I am ashamed that I let him make me feel that way. I somehow felt he was so awesome, and whatever he said, I thought that was the way it was. Near the end of our relationship, he would say and do things to make me feel terrible. I felt like I needed to get away, but I couldn't let go. I needed him for my happiness and my self-confidence. I never thought I would be this way about someone, but when you trust someone so much and tell them everything, it is hard not to feel like you are nothing without them.

I still have some of these feelings when I talk to Ethan, but now I am beginning to feel that I don't need someone else to be happy. Only I can make myself feel happy or sad.

–Jill, Age 17

I Need You

STORIES—PAGE 2

Adam's Story

When I first started going with Nikki, everything was great. We had a lot of fun together and never argued about anything. We were together all the time, and when we weren't, we were talking on the phone or sending notes to each other. The first time we had a fight was when she said she'd call me one night and she didn't. I just sat by the phone waiting for her to call, and finally I called her. Her brother said she wasn't home, and I really got upset, wondering where she could be and who she was with. By the time she finally did call, I was convinced she'd been out with someone else, and I was so jealous. She swore she was just riding around with her girlfriend and said she had every right to do that. I told her that I thought she always wanted to be with me, and she said she needed some time with her friends, too. I didn't understand that because I couldn't have much fun if I wasn't with her. We argued some more, and she finally hung up on me. My parents made me get off the phone, but I was so upset that I hardly slept all night. I kept wondering what I would do if she started doing more with her friends and didn't want to see me as much.

The next day at school she ignored me, and that night she went out with her friends again. I was furious. I followed them in my car, and Nikki finally got in and rode around with me. She told me that we had been spending way too much time together and that we should be with our friends more. I told her I couldn't stand not seeing her as much as we had been, and she said I needed to stop relying on her to do things with. I couldn't take it. I told her to get out of the car, and I left.

I didn't know what to do. The only reason I went to school was to see Nikki. She was all I thought about. I didn't want to be with my friends without her because I just kept thinking about what she might be doing. I was scared to death she would go out with someone else, and I didn't think I could stand that.

Things just kept getting worse. The more I begged to be with her, the more she pushed me away. I got really depressed and sometimes got drunk because I couldn't stand the pain. Every time I would see her at a party or talking to another guy, I'd go nuts. One night I decked a guy she had been talking to, and I got suspended from school for fighting with some guys who were talking to her in the hall.

I Need You

STORIES–PAGE 3

My parents were fed up with my behavior and told me to get over her. As if it were that easy. They wouldn't let me have any contact with her except at school. I just didn't know how I could go on without her; it was because of her that I could feel so good.

It took a long time for me to get over this. I went to counseling a few times. Sometimes I could be strong and think I could make it without her, but other times I just felt like I had to have her in my life. Finally, I can get through most days without thinking about her, and I try to avoid being places where I know she will be. My friends say that I need to get my own life, and I am trying to do that.

–Adam, Age 17

I Wish They Were Different

Developmental Perspective

The increased time adolescents spend with peers gives them opportunities to try on various roles; to learn to tolerate individual differences as they come in contact with people who have different attitudes, values, and life-styles; and to learn more about themselves in relation to others. In many instances, adolescents experience frustration because they want others to change to conform to their expectations.

Objective

▷ To learn what one can and cannot control in relationships with others

Materials

▷ Paper and pencil for each student

Procedure

1. Introduce the lesson by asking each student to think about a relationship with a parent or stepparent and a relationship with a peer. Have students identify two things about each relationship that they really appreciate and two things they would really like to change about each person. Ask them to write this information on their papers without revealing the names of the individuals.

2. Elicit some discussion about what students appreciate in others and what they would like to change. Ask how many of them have been successful at changing others, and how they feel when they can't do so.

3. Read the following to illustrate what people say to themselves and how they act when they think someone else's behavior or attitudes should change:

   Example: You think your parents should let you stay out until 2:00 A.M. They won't listen to your reasons. You are angry because you think they should see it your way. Because you think you are right, you stay out until 2:00 anyway, and then you get even angrier when they ground you. Any attempts to try and change them fail, and you end up in more trouble each time you try.

   Example: You hate it when your friends say they will call you or come over at a certain time and they don't. You think they should do what they say they will. The more you complain to them about it, the more you all end up arguing. Trying to change them isn't working.

In each example, the young person thought the other person should change, but the more he or she tried to control this, the more conflict there was. Usually, when you have a "should," you think the other person is acting in a way that isn't fair or right, and you think you need to correct the "injustice." Unfortunately, the other person also feels he or she is right, and when you try to control, he or she gets angry about that, so conflict usually develops. If you changed your "should" to a *preference* (I wish they would let me stay out until 2:00; I wish they would call or come over when they say they will), you are less likely to be upset and more likely to request change in a better way. For example, instead of complaining to your friends, you could deliver an assertive message: "I would appreciate it if you could call or come over when you say you will." That way, the other person is less likely to get defensive and angry but still has the right to change or not change. Ultimately, you have to ask yourself whom you can control: yourself and your thoughts and feelings, or another person. Sometimes, the more you try to control, the more you end up being controlled by your negative feelings.

4. Have students form groups of four and discuss the issue of controlling others: Is it possible? What are the consequences? What happens to your feelings when you try to control? and so on. Ask each group, by the end of the discussion, to generate a motto or a bumper sticker about the issue of controlling others. Allow the groups to share these.

5. Discuss the Content and Personalization Questions.

Discussion

CONTENT QUESTIONS

1. Do you think you can or cannot control others?
2. If you cannot control others, what can you control?
3. What do you have to think in order to give up the control?

PERSONALIZATION QUESTIONS

1. How do you feel when others try to control you? How do you attempt to deal with it?
2. Do you try to control others? If so, how does this usually work out for you?
3. What, if anything, would you like to change about your issues regarding controlling others?

Follow-up Activity

Have each student interview two adults, asking them about the issues of control discussed in this lesson. Ask each student to write at least four "I learned" statements to share with the group.

Dating "Do's" & "Don'ts"

Developmental Perspective

Although some teenagers start dating earlier, more serious dating generally begins after age 15, with relationships characterized by deep emotional involvement developing even later. Regardless of age, many adolescents lack the maturity to deal successfully with an intimate relationship, which may very likely involve being sexually active.

Objective

▷ To examine feelings and issues involving intimate relationships

Materials

▷ A copy of the Dating "Do's" and "Don'ts"–Checklist (Handout 8) for each student

▷ Pencil and paper for each student

Procedure

1. Introduce the lesson by asking each student to take out a sheet of paper and quickly write the first three words that come to mind when he or she thinks about dating relationships. (Stress that students will have the choice to share their responses or keep them private.) Ask willing students to share what words came to mind.

2. Mention that dating relationships are often characterized by both positive and negative feelings, and explain that students will receive a checklist that will give them an opportunity to think more carefully about some issues involved in intimate relationships. Distribute the Dating "Do's" and "Don'ts"–Checklist (Handout 8) to each student, and allow students time to complete it. Explain that they may keep their responses confidential and that they can respond to these items regardless of whether or not they are in dating relationships.

3. Break students into triads, and invite them to discuss whichever items on the checklist they feel comfortable discussing.

4. Discuss the Content and Personalization Questions.

Discussion

CONTENT QUESTIONS

1. What was it like for you to complete this checklist? Are the items on the checklist issues that you have thought about before?

2. Did you have more "agree," "disagree," or "undecided" responses?

PERSONALIZATION QUESTIONS

1. Think about which of these issues is the most difficult for you to deal with. Is it more difficult to address these issues if you are in a dating relationship than if you are just thinking about them hypothetically? (Invite discussion.)

2. If you are in a dating relationship, how happy are you with the relationship and your role in it? Is there anything you would like to change? If so, how do you anticipate doing this?

Follow-up Activity

Have students write "Dear Ann Landers" letters about dating relationship problems they currently have, have had, or anticipate having (including not being in a relationship but wanting to be). Have them respond to their own letters, giving themselves advice.

Dating "Do's" & "Don'ts"

CHECKLIST

Name: _____ Date: _____

Instructions: Respond to each item by circling A (agree), D (disagree), or U (undecided).
You may choose to keep your answers confidential.

A   D   U   1. I think couples who date should spend all their time together.

A   D   U   2. I think it's OK for couples who are dating to be sexually active in high school.

A   D   U   3. I think couples who date should be jealous if each partner has a close friend of the opposite sex.

A   D   U   4. I think people who date should change their values and beliefs to conform to those of their partners.

A   D   U   5. I think it's OK for couples who are dating to kiss and hug each other at school.

A   D   U   6. I think people who are dating should put the needs of their partners ahead of their own.

A   D   U   7. I think people who are dating should dress to please their partners.

A   D   U   8. I think people who are dating should put their interests and hobbies aside and do what their partners like.

A   D   U   9. If one partner wants to be sexually active and threatens to break up if the other one won't, I think the partner who doesn't want to should give in rather than risk ending the relationship.

A   D   U   10. I think it is all right for couples who have just begun dating to be sexually active.

Romantic Relationships

Developmental Perspective

Although many serious dating relationships don't begin until after age 15, many adolescents have their own concept of "going with" someone, even if it only involves contact on the phone and at school. These relationships are often very intense and can be a source of pain as well as pleasure. Because adolescents often have difficulty handling intense emotions, it is easy for them to become overwhelmed and depressed about romantic relationships.

Objectives

▷ To explore feelings about romantic relationships

▷ To learn to distinguish between healthy and unhealthy ways of dealing with issues pertaining to romantic relationships

Materials

▷ A chalkboard

▷ A copy of the Romantic Relationships–Poem (Handout 9) for each student

▷ Paper and pencil for each student

Procedure

1. Introduce the lesson by engaging students in a discussion about what it means to be in a romantic relationship. Ask them to identify both the positive and negative aspects of this involvement. Then ask students to brainstorm feelings associated with romantic relationships and write them on paper. Invite sharing with the total group, and record the words on the board.

2. Ask students to list three healthy ways to deal with feelings when a romantic relationship is confusing and conflictual, followed by three unhealthy ways. Write the headings "healthy" and "unhealthy" on the board, and under each heading, list what students have identified. Engage them in a discussion of the differences between healthy and unhealthy ways to deal with feelings in such a situation.

3. Distribute the Romantic Relationships–Poem (Handout 9) to each student. Ask students to read the poem and write short reactions.

4. Discuss the Content and Personalization Questions.

Discussion

CONTENT QUESTIONS

     1. What are some of the feelings the writer of this poem was experiencing?

     2. What do you think this poem means?

PERSONALIZATION QUESTIONS

     1. Have you or has someone you know ever experienced feelings like this?

     2. If you have experienced feelings like this, how have you dealt with them? Do you think that you handled them in a healthy or an unhealthy way?

Follow-up Activity

Invite students to write their own poems or stories about involvement in romantic relationships that they have had or wish they had.

Romantic Relationships

POEM

Name: _____ Date: _____

Instructions: Read the poem and write a brief reaction to it. What do you think the writer was experiencing in this relationship?

Letting my feelings get in the way.

I always try not to feel.

But I'm scared.

Scared that I'm beginning to care in a different way.

Scared of losing you someday.

Scared that I feel stronger than you.

Scared that after all this time you may just decide
I'm nothing you thought I was.

I want you to know me.

I want you to tell me your thoughts.

I want you to hold me.

I want to be there for you on your coldest,
darkest night.

The past has made me regret, and I hope
it doesn't get in the way.

But if it does, I know it is my fault.
I didn't see what was really there, did I?

–Leia, Age 16

Predict the Outcome

Developmental Perspective

Although adolescents at this stage are continuing to develop their abstract thinking skills, many still lack the ability to predict outcomes of their choices. Since they are making increasingly difficult decisions, it is important for them to learn how to anticipate consequences.

Objective

▷ To learn to predict the outcomes of choices

Materials

▷ A balloon and a straight pin

▷ A copy of the Predict the Outcome–Worksheet (Handout 10) and a pencil for each student

Procedure

1. Introduce the lesson by blowing up a balloon and tying it. Ask students what will happen if you stick the pin in the balloon. After they answer, pop the balloon. Then discuss the concept of predicting outcomes as an important aspect of the decision-making process. Emphasize the importance of taking into account probabilities in predicting consequences of actions.

2. Distribute the Predict the Outcome–Worksheet (Handout 10) to each student. Have students predict two possible outcomes for each of the choices on the worksheet.

3. Have students break into triads to discuss their outcomes.

4. Discuss the Content and Personalization Questions.

Discussion

CONTENT QUESTIONS

1. How did you decide on the outcomes you predicted for the examples on the worksheet?

2. Do you think you can make better decisions if you can predict the outcomes? Why or why not?

3. Do you think it is possible always to predict outcomes?

PERSONALIZATION QUESTIONS

1. Do you typically try to predict outcomes for decisions you make? If so, do you think this helps you? If you don't, how do you think this affects your life?

2. Think about yourself five years from now. What do you think will be the most important decision you'll make? Do you think it will be important to predict possible outcomes for this decision? (Invite discussion.)

Follow-up Activity

Ask each student to identify a decision he or she will need to make during the next year. Ask students to select two possible courses of action for their decisions and write short papers predicting the outcome for each option.

Predict the Outcome

WORKSHEET

Name: _____ Date: _____

Instructions: Read the choices, and write two possible outcomes for each one.

Choices

1. You go to college.

2. You get married when you are 18.

3. You drop out of high school.

4. You join the army, navy, or marines.

5. You join a gang.

6. You become addicted to drugs.

7. You have an abortion.

8. You run away from home because you are angry with your parent(s).

9. You become addicted to cigarettes.

10. You start dealing drugs to make money.

11. You become a parent at age 16 and keep the baby.

12. You rob a convenience store.

13. (Add your own.) _____ _____

14. (Add your own.) _____ _____

Possible outcomes

1. A. _____
   B. _____

2. A. _____
   B. _____

3. A. _____
   B. _____

4. A. _____
   B. _____

5. A. _____
   B. _____

6. A. _____
   B. _____

7. A. _____
   B. _____

8. A. _____
   B. _____

9. A. _____
   B. _____

10. A. _____
    B. _____

11. A. _____
    B. _____

12. A. _____
    B. _____

13. A. _____
    B. _____

14. A. _____
    B. _____

Make a Plan

Developmental Perspective

Because many adolescents at this stage still live in the here and now, they have difficulty thinking ahead and setting goals. However, because they are about to enter a transitional period in life and must make decisions about the future, it is critical for them to learn how to make realistic plans that lead to goal attainment.

Objective

▷ To learn how to make realistic plans

Materials

▷ A copy of the Make a Plan–Worksheet (Handout 11) and a pencil for each student

Procedure

1. Introduce the lesson by quoting the saying "If you don't know where you're going, you'll end up somewhere else" and asking students to contemplate implications for themselves at this point in their lives.

2. Discuss the concept of long-range and short-range plans, emphasizing the points covered in the Developmental Perspective.

3. Distribute the Make a Plan–Worksheet (Handout 11) to each student. Have students fill in each step of the plan with personal examples as you explain the process.

4. Discuss the Content and Personalization Questions.

Discussion

CONTENT QUESTIONS

1. Which part of the plan seems the most doable? The least doable?

2. What do you think stops people from making plans or following through on them?

3. Do you think it is a good idea to use a process like the one on the worksheet? If so, how do you think it could be helpful?

PERSONALIZATION QUESTIONS

1. Do you think you will put your plan into action? If not, what do you think will prevent you from doing this?

2. Do you typically make plans to change things that need to be changed? If not, do you think this process might be helpful to you?

3. Many people feel less overwhelmed once they have identified small steps as part of a bigger plan. Does this apply to you—do you feel less overwhelmed when you identify small steps?

Follow-up Activity

Have each student take another issue he or she wants to work on and follow the steps of the plan. Encourage students to report back on how the process worked for them.

Make a Plan

WORKSHEET–PAGE 1

Name: _____ Date: _____

Instructions: Complete each step, using your own examples.

Step 1

Identify three things that are going well in your life.

1. _____

2. _____

3. _____

Step 2

Identify three things that you would like to change . . . things that aren't going well.

1. _____

2. _____

3. _____

Step 3

Take each of the three things you'd like to change and assign it to one of the following categories (or create your own):

1. Relationships with friends or teachers

2. School

3. Relationships with family members

4. Money, job

5. Future plans

Make a Plan

WORKSHEET–PAGE 2

Step 4

For each category, identify something very specific you would like to change. For example, if in Step 2 you said you wanted to have a better relationship with your boyfriend or girlfriend, you would categorize that under number 1, "relationships with friends." A specific might be seeing each other more often.

Need to change: _____

Need to change: _____

Need to change: _____

Step 5

Make a specific, doable plan. For example, if you wanted to see someone more often, your doable plan could be to continue going out on Friday or Saturday and also to meet for at least an hour on Tuesday or Wednesday after work.

Doable plan: _____

Doable plan: _____

Doable plan: _____

Make a Plan

WORKSHEET–PAGE 3

Step 6

List any barriers to your plan: What might prevent it from succeeding? Predict the barriers, and list suggestions for overcoming them. For example, a barrier to seeing each other on Tuesday or Wednesday might be having too much homework. A suggestion for overcoming that barrier would be to study together or to meet for only 30 minutes.

Possible barrier:_____

Suggestion: _____

Possible barrier:_____

Suggestion: _____

Possible barrier:_____

Suggestion: _____

Step 7

Put the plan into action!

Rational Thinking

Developmental Perspective

At this stage, there are still many inconsistencies in adolescents' ability to use common sense and make good decisions. Some adolescents are still quite concrete in their thinking and see things dichotomously. They can still easily become overwhelmed and blow things out of proportion, and this has negative impact on various aspects of their lives.

Objectives

▷ To learn rational thinking skills

▷ To learn how to apply rational thinking skills to one's life

Materials

▷ A copy of the Rational Thinking–Worksheet (Handout 12) for each student

▷ Pencil and paper for each student

Procedure

1. Introduce the lesson by explaining the difference between rational and irrational thinking:

   Rational thinking is based on realistic expectations and helps you attain goals. Irrational thinking does not help you attain goals because you are overwhelmed by disturbing emotions such as anger, guilt, or depression, which result from thinking irrational thoughts. There are three basic types of irrational beliefs:

   ▶ "Shoulds," or demands for others or for yourself: believing that others should always treat you exactly as you think you should be treated

   ▶ Self-downing: equating who you are with what you do (if you don't perform well you think you are a worthless person)

   ▶ Low frustration tolerance: thinking that everything should be easy for you, that you shouldn't have to tolerate any frustration or discomfort in your life

   In addition, people who think irrationally "awfulize" and overgeneralize. They blow things out of proportion and assume the absolute worst. They also may use what is called tunnel vision, taking a small detail and using it as the basis for making all other judgments. Or they may make arbitrary inferences, assuming something even when there is no basis for it. All-or-nothing thinking is also very common: Things are either one way or the other; there is no in-between.

Following are examples of irrational thinking:

- ► My boyfriend should always call me exactly when he says he will. If he doesn't, it must mean that he's going to break up with me, that I'm not good enough for him, and that he's a real jerk. If he breaks up with me, I won't be able to stand it.

- ► This algebra teacher is so boring, and the work is way too hard. I'm just going to drop the course because I can never put up with this.

- ► If my parents don't let me have the car tonight, I will run away. They are so strict with me, and they never let me do anything. They should be like everyone else's parents.

2. Distribute the Rational Thinking–Worksheet (Handout 12) to each student. Have students identify the irrational beliefs and indicate what is irrational about them.

3. Introduce the concept of disputing as a way to dispel irrational beliefs. Disputing involves asking oneself challenging questions that poke holes in the illogical reasoning that characterizes irrational beliefs. Present the following example:

- ► A (Activating Event): You didn't score well on the ACT or SAT exam.

- ► B (Irrational Beliefs): You think, "How stupid I am. I'll never get into college with this score. Why can't I ever do anything right? I probably won't do any better if I take it again, so I might as well just give up and forget about college."

- ► C (Emotional Consequence): You feel depressed and disgusted with yourself.

- ► D (Dispute): Challenge your thoughts. Ask yourself: "Just because I didn't do well on this exam, where is the evidence that I'm stupid? Just because I did poorly, it doesn't necessarily mean I can't get into any college. Also, colleges look at other things besides SAT and ACT scores. I didn't do well this time, but where is the evidence that I won't do better if I take the test again?"

- ► E (New Effect): As a result of the disputing, you have a better perspective on the problem, and you can employ more effective problem-solving skills. You are not as down on yourself. You recognize that one bad score might not have the disastrous consequences you originally assumed when you were reacting irrationally.

4. Ask students to identify examples of their own irrational thinking and work through the A-B-C-D-E model to dispute their irrational beliefs.

5. Discuss the Content and Personalization Questions.

Discussion

CONTENT QUESTIONS

1. How would you describe the difference between rational and irrational thinking?
2. How easy was it for you to identify the irrational beliefs on the worksheet?
3. Do you think irrational thinking is common?

PERSONALIZATION QUESTIONS

1. Do you believe you tend to think more rationally or irrationally?
2. Which type of thinking do you believe will help you achieve your goals and handle problems most effectively?
3. Is there anything you need to change about the way you think in order to handle situations more effectively? If so, what? How will you make the changes?
4. Did you learn anything from this lesson that you can apply to your life? (Invite sharing.)

Follow-up Activity

Encourage each student to identify an activating event and work through the A-B-C-D-E model. Allow time for students to report back on this process and help them refine their skills in employing it.

Rational Thinking

WORKSHEET–PAGE 1

Name: _____ Date: _____

Instructions: Read the following thinking patterns, and identify the irrational beliefs (IRB's).

1. I'm going to quit this job. It's too hard to learn all the things I have to do.

    IRB's _____

    _____

2. I have way too much to do in the next week. I'll never get it done, and I'll do a bad job on it anyway.

    IRB's _____

    _____

3. I can't stand it if my girlfriend (or boyfriend) breaks up with me. I'll never find anyone like her (or him) again.

    IRB's _____

    _____

4. If I don't make the first-string basketball team, it will prove what a loser I am.

    IRB's _____

    _____

5. My parents never let me do anything. Everyone else has more freedom than I do.

    IRB's _____

    _____

Rational Thinking

WORKSHEET–PAGE 2

6. I know I flunked that advanced algebra test. I'm so stupid. I'll probably get a *D* in the course, and that will just prove how dumb I really am.

    IRB's _____

    _____

7. I can't stand my French teacher. She never explains anything, and she expects us to understand the assignments. I'm just going to stop trying because it's too frustrating.

    IRB's _____

    _____

8. I didn't get into the National Honor Society. I should have studied harder, but it probably wouldn't have made any difference–I don't have anything going for me.

    IRB's _____

    _____

9. I'm going to break up with my boyfriend. He shouldn't be so inconsiderate. He always goes out with his friends and never pays any attention to me. I think he should be with me the majority of the time.

    IRB's _____

    _____

10. I hate this town. Everything about it is awful. As soon as I graduate I'm out of here.

    IRB's _____

    _____

Evaluating Decisions

Developmental Perspective

At a time in their lives when adolescents increasingly face important decisions, the ability to evaluate these decisions is a critical skill.

Objective

▷ To learn to evaluate decisions

Materials

▷ A copy of the Evaluating Decisions–Situations (Handout 13) for each student

▷ Paper and pencil for each student

Procedure

1. Introduce the lesson by distributing a copy of the Evaluating Decisions–Situations (Handout 13) to each student. Then break students into triads, and assign one of the situations to each group. Have students read their situations; list the decisions; and discuss whether the decisions made were good, fair, or poor. They should also state the reasons for their evaluations.

2. After sufficient discussion time, have each group share the results of their discussion. Emphasize the fact that a decision made at one point in time can affect subsequent decisions or outcomes.

3. Ask each group to identify a decision one of the members has made recently. They should discuss whether this decision affected other decisions and how they would evaluate this decision.

4. Discuss the Content and Personalization Questions.

Discussion

CONTENT QUESTIONS

1. How did you decide whether the decisions were good, fair, or poor?

2. In the situations on the worksheet or in your own examples, did decisions made at one point in time affect other outcomes?

PERSONALIZATION QUESTIONS

1. How would you evaluate the majority of your decisions—good, fair, or poor?

2. Before you make a decision, do you think about the outcome and the impact it might have on other decisions?

3. Is there anything you think you need to change about your decision-making process? If so, what will you do to change it?

4. What did you learn from this lesson that might be helpful to you in making decisions?

Follow-up Activity

Have students listen to popular songs and list some of the choices that are described in the lyrics. Ask them to evaluate whether these are good, fair, or poor choices and explain why they evaluated them as they did.

Evaluating Decisions

SITUATIONS-PAGE 1

Instructions: Read the situation assigned to your group. List all the decisions you see in the situation. Rate each decision as good, fair, or poor–and give a reason for each rating.

Situation 1

Seth had an old car that needed new tires, a clutch, and new brakes. The tape player didn't work, and the car was beginning to rust. Seth had been saving money for the repairs, but he had only managed to save 100 dollars because he had to spend money for the prom: the limo, dinner and breakfast in expensive restaurants, his tux, and tickets to the dance. In addition, he had bought two tickets to a concert that would take place the following week. Now the problem was that Seth had no way of getting to the concert. He couldn't drive his car out of town in the shape it was in, and his girlfriend didn't have a car. To complicate the situation further, he found out that his big term paper in U.S. history was due the day after the concert. He hadn't even started it, and it was 50 percent of his grade.

Seth didn't want to miss the concert, so he started asking friends if he could borrow a car or ride with someone who was going. He finally found a way to get there if he paid for the gas. That sounded OK to Seth since his payday would be the day before the concert. The only problem was that gas was going to cost more for his friend's car than for his own, so he'd have less money for the week. Oh, well–he'd worry about that later. Now he just had to figure out how to get the history paper done. He was scheduled to work all weekend, but maybe he could just call in sick and work on the paper then. His boss wouldn't like it, but . . . he didn't think he'd get fired just because he missed a few days of work. The only problem was that he'd done the same thing last month.

Decisions:_____

_____

_____

_____

Evaluating Decisions

SITUATIONS–PAGE 2

Situation 2

Carla had been working at McDonald's all year, but her boss was giving her a bad time about taking time off for track practice. He informed her that she would have to work Saturday nights until closing. That really upset Carla. It was her junior year, and Saturday night was the only night she could really go out and party with her friends. She needed the money because she had to start saving for college and had to pay off some layaway bills. But–she wasn't about to work on Saturday nights or put up with the hassle from her boss. She had to quit.

Carla's mother was not happy with her decision and told Carla she did not have the money to help her with all of her upcoming expenses. So Carla started looking for another job. She found one where she could work from 6:00 to 10:00 P.M. Monday through Thursday. That was perfect, except that she had to do all of her studying after she got home at night. On a particular day she was worried because she somehow had to find time to study for a big Spanish test and write a paper for English. She now regretted that the previous night after work she had gone over to her boyfriend's house instead of writing the paper. She also had to find time in the next week to finish two college applications.

That night Carla got off work late and went home, intending to study for the exam and write the paper. But just as she walked in the door, her boyfriend called, and they talked a long time. Then she took a shower, and it was 11:30 when she started to work on the paper. She finished at 1:00 A.M. and was too tired to study for the exam. Carla set her alarm for 6:00 A.M., but she must have slept through it because when she woke up she had only 30 minutes to get dressed and get to school. She knew she didn't do well on the exam. It worried her because she had to keep her grades up in order to have a good chance at scholarships for the next year.

Decisions:_____

_____

_____

_____

the **PASSPORT** PROGRAM

GRADE 12

Self-Development
ACTIVITY
1 Self-Assessment
2 Roles I Play
3 Self-Abuse
4 Me and My Future

Emotional Development
ACTIVITY
1 It Hurts to Be in Love
2 I'm Lonely
3 Ambivalence
4 Troubling Transitions

Social Development
ACTIVITY
1 Please Pick Me
2 Saying Goodbye
3 Love You, Love You Not
4 Parameters with Parents

Cognitive Development
ACTIVITY
1 It's a Dilemma
2 Goals Galore
3 Big Decisions
4 Priorities, Please

Self-Assessment

Developmental Perspective

As adolescents leave high school, the way they assess themselves is affected by the transition. Those who are self-confident handle this change with ease, but it is not at all uncommon for them to feel some anxiety about who they are and how they will measure up in new environments.

Objective

▷ To assess personal strengths

Materials

▷ A copy of the Self-Assessment–Worksheet (Handout 1) and a pencil for each student

Procedure

1. Introduce the lesson by discussing the fact that students' assessments of themselves may change as they make the transition from high school and encounter new people and new circumstances. Explain that the purpose of this lesson is to help them identify personal strengths and indicators of those strengths.

2. Distribute the Self-Assessment–Worksheet (Handout 1) to each student. Ask students to complete it.

3. Have students form groups of four to share their self-assessments.

4. Discuss the Content and Personalization Questions.

Discussion

CONTENT QUESTIONS

1. Was it difficult to select the five terms that best described you? How was it for you to think of the indicators?

2. How did you select the terms that least characterized you? How did you feel about those selections?

PERSONALIZATION QUESTIONS

1. Of the characteristics you selected for your "top five" list, which ones do you think will be the biggest assets to you as you move into the next stage of your life?

2. Of the characteristics you selected for your "bottom five" list, which ones do you think you might want to work on to help you be more successful in the future?

3. Which personal characteristics are you most proud of?

Follow-up Activity

Invite each student to select one or two personal characteristics he or she would like to develop and make a realistic plan to do so.

Self-Assessment

WORKSHEET

Name: _____ Date: _____

Instructions: Read the words and phrases on this worksheet. First, put the number 1 to the left of the five terms that best describe you. Next to each of the terms, write an indicator of the way you demonstrate that behavior in your life. Second, put the number 2 beside five terms that also describe you, although not as well as the first five. Write indicators for these terms as well. Finally, select a third set of five terms that don't describe you very well. For these, write indicators that describe why these terms are not very characteristic of you. (For example, if you are not shy, an indicator would be that you meet people easily and are the life of the party.)

_____ Responsible_____

_____ Easy to get along with _____

_____ Dependable_____

_____ Organized _____

_____ Fun to be with _____

_____ Shy/quiet_____

_____ Makes friends easily _____

_____ Perfectionistic_____

_____ Even-tempered_____

_____ Goal-oriented_____

_____ Nonjudgmental _____

_____ Tolerant _____

_____ Self-confident_____

_____ Relates well to others _____

_____ Creative _____

Roles I Play

Developmental Perspective

As adolescents reach the end of high school, the roles they currently assume will change as they become more independent and move into a different phase of life. Helping them develop some understanding of this change process increases their self-awareness.

Objective

▷ To identify present and future roles

Materials

▷ Paper and pencil for each student

▷ An envelope of Roles I Play–Definitions (Handout 2) for each group of four students

Procedure

1. Introduce the lesson by discussing the fact that as students leave high school, many of them will be moving away, continuing their schooling, getting married, or getting jobs in other locations. Explain that as they move into these new situations, the roles they have played throughout high school will change.

2. Have students form groups of four, and have each group appoint a recorder. Distribute an envelope of Roles I Play–Definitions (Handout 2) to each group. Ask them to draw out the slips, one at a time, and discuss how they see themselves changing in the next year or two relative to the indicated role. The recorder should summarize the group's ideas about each role.

3. Discuss the Content and Personalization Questions.

Discussion

CONTENT QUESTIONS

1. On the basis of your responses during the discussion, are there any roles that you don't think will change?

2. Are there any entirely new roles you think you will assume as you move into the next stage of your life? (Invite sharing.)

PERSONALIZATION QUESTIONS

1. Which roles do you think will change the most for you?
   How do you feel about that?

2. Which roles do you think will change the least for you?
   How do you feel about that?

3. What did you learn as a result of this discussion?

Follow-up Activity

Invite a group of last year's graduates to speak to the group about ways their roles changed and new roles they had to assume.

Roles I Play

DEFINITIONS

Leader note: Copy and cut apart; give each group of four students an envelope containing one set of role definitions. Put several blank slips in each envelope for students to add their own.

Son or daughter	Musician
Boyfriend or girlfriend	Grandson or granddaughter
Best friend	Member of a church or synagogue
Student	Member of a community
Athlete	Sibling

Self-Abuse

Developmental Perspective

Although many adolescents are generally more self-confident at this stage than they were during early adolescence, self-respect can be a problem. In numerous ways, young people abuse themselves or tolerate abusive behaviors from others; this in turn results in negative feelings and attitudes towards themselves.

Objectives

▷ To distinguish between abuse and self-abuse

▷ To identify strategies to deal with self-abusive behaviors or abusive behaviors inflicted by others

Materials

▷ A chalkboard

▷ Paper and pencil for each student

▷ Multiple copies of short informative articles on the following topics: physical abuse, emotional abuse, sexual abuse, date rape, anorexia, bulimia, substance abuse

Procedure

1. Introduce the lesson by writing the words *abuse* and *self-abuse* on the board. Ask students to discuss the meaning of these terms and to give some examples of each. Discuss the difference between abuse that is inflicted by oneself and abuse that is inflicted by others. Ask students about which type of abuse they feel would be most difficult to deal with.

2. Divide students into seven small groups, and ask each group to select one of the seven topics. Then give each student in each group a copy of the article that corresponds to the group's topic.

3. Allow time for reading of the articles, and ask each group to prepare a brief summary of the information to present to the total group. Next, have each person in each group identify two possible strategies for dealing with the problems associated with the topic. Have each group discuss the proposed strategies and arrive at a consensus on the three best suggestions.

4. Reconvene the total group so each small group can briefly summarize their topic and present their preferred strategies.

5. Discuss the Content and Personalization Questions.

Discussion

CONTENT QUESTIONS

1. How do you distinguish between self-abuse and other types of abuse?

2. What did you learn about your topic or other topics that you hadn't known before?

3. Do you think it is possible for people who have been abused by others to stop being victims and gain control of their lives? If so, how?

PERSONALIZATION QUESTIONS

1. What do you think you can do to prevent yourself from being a victim of physical, emotional, or sexual abuse? Date rape?

2. If you have experienced any of those things, does it mean you are a bad person? Should you respect yourself any less just because someone else didn't respect you?

3. If you or someone you know inflicts self-abuse through starvation, binging and purging, or substance abuse, what would it take for you or that person to demonstrate enough self-respect to stop?

Follow-up Activity

Invite guest speakers to talk about the lesson topics and outline what young people can do to prevent abuse or to empower themselves if they are victims of abuse by others.

Me & My Future

Developmental Perspective

During this stage of development, adolescents experience increasing pressure to define who they are and what they want to do when they grow up. For many, this is a perplexing question. Adolescents often experience anxiety and confusion because they feel compelled to "figure it out." Although it is important for adolescents to have some sense of direction, they mature at different rates, so some may be better able to look at themselves and their futures than others.

Objective

▷ To clarify how one sees oneself in the future

Materials

▷ A copy of the Me and My Future–Rank-Order Worksheet (Handout 3) and a pencil for each student

Procedure

1. Introduce the lesson by discussing the fact that students are reaching a point in their development where they are naturally beginning to think about who they are and how they see themselves in the future.

2. Distribute the Me and My Future–Rank-Order Worksheet (Handout 3) to each student. Ask students to think seriously about how they see themselves in the future and to complete the worksheet.

3. Allow time for students to discuss their rankings in small groups.

4. Discuss the Content and Personalization Questions.

Discussion

CONTENT QUESTIONS

1. Was it difficult to rank the items on the worksheet? If so, what about the process was difficult?

2. Which issues did you have to think about the most?

3. Are there other issues that you think should have been included on this list? (Invite sharing.)

PERSONALIZATION QUESTIONS

1. What did you learn about yourself by doing this activity?

2. If you had completed this worksheet a year ago, do you think your rankings would have been the same? Why or why not? If you were to do this again in another year, how do you think your rankings might change?

3. When you think about the future, what is your image of yourself?

4. How do you feel when you think about your future?

Follow-up Activity

Invite students to make posters depicting how they see themselves in the future.

Me & My Future

RANK—ORDER WORKSHEET

Name: _____ Date: _____

Instructions: Read the items in the list. Number them from 1 to 15 (1 = most like me, 15 = least like me) on the basis of how you see yourself in the future.

_____ Living near my parent(s)

_____ Actively practicing my religion

_____ Living in a big metropolitan area

_____ Having a prestigious job

_____ Living in the community where I grew up

_____ Joining the service (army, navy, marines, air force)

_____ Living for at least a while in a foreign country

_____ Getting a job right after high school

_____ Living in a racially and ethnically diverse community

_____ Going to a two-year vocational school

_____ Living in a small town

_____ Getting married before I'm 20

_____ Going to college

_____ Earning a big salary

_____ Becoming a parent before I'm 20

It Hurts to Be in Love

Developmental Perspective

Romantic relationships are the source of intense, oftentimes painful emotions during this period of adolescent development. Because females tend to develop romantic interests earlier than males, they also suffer more disillusionment when the realities of intimate relationships do not match up with their fantasies of romance. Adolescents need to learn effective coping strategies for dealing with these issues.

Objectives

▷ To identify feelings connected with romantic relationships

▷ To distinguish between healthy and unhealthy ways of coping with these emotions

Materials

▷ A chalkboard

▷ A copy of It Hurts to Be in Love–Poem (Handout 4) for each student

▷ Paper and pencil for each student

Procedure

1. Introduce the lesson by discussing its objectives. Distribute the It Hurts to Be in Love–Poem (Handout 4) to each student. When students have finished reading the poem, ask them to write three feelings that were mentioned or alluded to in the poem as well as their reactions to the content.

2. Break students into groups of four, and have them discuss the feelings expressed in the poem and their reactions.

3. Ask each student to identify three things he or she has tried or thinks would be effective for dealing with painful relationships. Have students share their suggestions in their small groups.

4. Discuss the Content and Personalization Questions.

Discussion

CONTENT QUESTIONS

1. What were some of your suggestions for dealing with painful feelings resulting from romantic relationships? (List suggestions on the board.)

2. What is the difference between coping in a healthy, effective way and coping in an unhealthy way? (Ask students to share examples of unhealthy ways of coping and to identify the negative effects of these methods.)

PERSONALIZATION QUESTIONS

1. Have you experienced feelings about a romantic relationship similar to those expressed in the poem?

2. If you have experienced a similar situation, how have you dealt with it? Do you think you coped in a healthy or an unhealthy way—or both?

3. Is there anything you think you can do to reduce the degree of painful emotion that often occurs in a romantic relationship?

Follow-up Activity

Invite students to write their own poems expressing their feelings about romantic or platonic relationships.

It Hurts to Be in Love

POEM

The thoughts that I had, things I should have shared or done . . . you'll never know.

The things that I feel, and now I deal, or at least try to hide the pain so that you'll never know; it could only add to your pride.

The lies that you told, the life that you faked, I miss it all, and I would take it back any day of this life,

This life that you've left, left me to live . . . by myself.

So alone with regrets, my tears are no more, no longer . . .

They've dried because I've cried myself to sleep every night, only to dream of you and wish for you, to only hold me tight for one last night

Or maybe even an hour of my lonely life.

Life lasts how long? I wonder every day when I think of you . . . or dream that it could be again, and maybe then I could be the person you need.

But no . . . not ever . . . no more chances, no more glances.

My heart only drops, only drops to know that you, strong you, will never think of me again or want to hold my hand.

Tell me I'm beautiful, lie to my face . . . hiding your love for not me, just her.

To know that it's her, the one that you dream of and live for, it's hard for me to bear.

Now I can only have you and hold you in my dreams, so I go to sleep hoping that one night I won't wake up because I know you'll never be next to me, to lie . . . to love . . . to hold in my arms.

Every day is an eternity away, away from what I want, away from what I feel I had, which is you.

To love me, to want me there in your life, to love and to cherish and to make me your wife.

Want me, hold me, say that you care, that you'll always be there to help me, to hold me, to help me stop this insanity that you've created in me, a hate for her and a constant jealousy.

To see you with her, with love, the love that I need; you'll never know how much that hurts.

But I need to live . . . or maybe I'll just cry, and then die—without you.

—Anika, Age 16

I'm Lonely

Developmental Perspective

Many adolescents, particularly high school seniors, feel lonely. They may be gradually growing away from their friends as their interests and beliefs change. Because many adolescents at this stage are becoming involved in significant dating relationships, those who aren't may feel different, isolated, and lonely.

Objectives

▷ To learn more about loneliness during adolescence

▷ To identify ways to deal with loneliness

Materials

▷ A copy of the I'm Lonely–Thoughts (Handout 5) for each student

▷ Paper and pencil for each student

Procedure

1. Discuss the fact that many students feel lonely as they enter the last year of high school because their interests and values are changing, they may be breaking away more from their parents, and they may feel lonely if they aren't in dating relationships while their friends are. In addition, point out that at this stage of development, many of them are ready to move on and meet new people, so they may associate less with friends they've had all through high school.

2. Distribute the I'm Lonely–Thoughts (Handout 5) to each student. Invite students to read the handout and respond to the questions at the end.

3. Have students form small groups to share their own experiences and their responses to the questions.

4. Discuss the Content and Personalization Questions.

Discussion

CONTENT QUESTIONS

1. Did you learn anything about feelings of loneliness from reading these thoughts?

2. Do you think these feelings are common during adolescence?

PERSONALIZATION QUESTIONS

1. Have you been aware of feeling more lonely during this past six months to a year?

2. If so, does it help to know that loneliness is a common feeling at this time in your life?

3. How do you deal with your lonely feelings?

Follow-up Activity

Encourage students to bring in songs that they listen to when they feel lonely or to write poems or stories to express these feelings.

I'm Lonely

THOUGHTS

Name: _____ Date: _____

Instructions: Read these thoughts, written by a real teenager, and respond to the questions at the end.

When I refer to feeling lonely, I mean that I feel alone. But being alone and feeling lonely are very different. I've felt lonely, on occasion, when I am alone, but it is not a severe feeling. I am perfectly happy being with my own thoughts. If I do feel this way, it is because I am remembering what it was like to have a real best friend who understood me well. Now I don't seem to have that. We've grown away from each other because our values have changed, I guess. But I really miss having that best friend, a kindred spirit.

At one point in time I lost respect for my peers. They wanted to do things that I didn't. They didn't understand the restrictions I put on myself. All in all, I grew away from them, and I guess that just happens. I'm a senior in high school, and I probably won't see these people very much later in life. I miss the cohesive group that we had, but that is over.

What I think creates the most problems now is not having a new group to fall into. In every class there are people that I should try to break down the barriers with so that I don't feel so alone. But that's hard. Slowly I am finding some people that enjoy "good, clean fun" again, and I'm beginning to develop some new friendships. But in reality, I think I will still feel this loneliness until I move away next year and have a chance to start over again.

–Katlin, High School Senior

Can you identify with Katlin's feelings? If so, what situations contributed to your feelings of loneliness?

_____

_____

When you have experienced these lonely feelings, what have you tried to do to help yourself deal with them?

_____

_____

Do you think it is common for young people your age to feel lonely because they are growing apart from their friends?

_____

_____

Ambivalence

Developmental Perspective

As adolescents enter the last years of high school, most experience ambivalent emotions: anxious to leave but scared to go, excited about the future but reluctant to let go of the past. Although schools prepare students with the necessary paperwork for getting out the door and on to the next stage of life, they often don't address the conflicting emotions that can be troublesome for adolescents.

Objective

▷ To identify ambivalent feelings common during the last two years of high school

Materials

▷ Paper and pencil for each student

▷ A copy of the Ambivalence–Sentence Starters (Handout 6) for each student

Procedure

1. Introduce the lesson by briefly discussing the meaning of the word *ambivalence*. Explain that the purpose of this lesson is to address the ambivalent feelings that are common during the last years of high school.

2. Distribute the Ambivalence–Sentence Starters (Handout 6) to each student. Ask students to complete the sentences.

3. When they are finished, invite discussion and sharing in small groups.

4. Discuss the Content and Personalization Questions.

Discussion

CONTENT QUESTIONS

1. Before this activity, were you aware of the range of ambivalent feelings?

2. Was it difficult for you to complete the sentences?

3. Which sentences were particularly difficult to complete?

4. On the basis of your responses, how would you summarize your feelings about moving on to the next phase of your life?

PERSONALIZATION QUESTIONS

1. Have you been experiencing ambivalence about high school coming to an end? Which ambivalent feelings have been most prevalent for you?

2. How do you deal with these feelings?

3. Did you learn anything today that might be helpful to you as you complete one stage of life and move on to another? (Invite sharing.)

Follow-up Activity

Have students write letters to themselves, reassuring themselves that these ambivalent feelings are normal and that it is helpful to talk about them or write journal entries about them.

Ambivalence

SENTENCE STARTERS

Name: _____ Date: _____

Instructions: Complete each sentence after reflecting on how it applies to you.

1. When I think about leaving high school, I feel _____
   _____

2. A good thing about leaving high school will be _____
   _____

3. Something that worries me about being out of high school is_____
   _____

4. When I think about leaving home, I feel _____
   _____

5. When I think about leaving my friends, I feel_____
   _____

6. If I'm not leaving this area, I feel _____
   _____

7. If I'm going to college, I feel _____
   _____

8. If I'm getting a job after high school, I feel _____
   _____

9. When I think about meeting new friends after I leave here, I feel_____
   _____

10. What I'll miss most about my life right now is _____
    _____

11. When I think about the future, I feel_____
    _____

12. If I don't know what I want to do after I graduate, I feel_____
    _____

Troubling Transitions

Developmental Perspective

With any transition, there is a change in roles, relationships, routines, and self-assessment. Graduation from high school is an important rite of passage that can have significant impact on adolescents. Preparing them to deal with this transition is an important part of facilitating their developmental journey.

Objectives

▷ To learn about the changes associated with transitions

▷ To identify how one's life will be affected by the transition out of high school

Materials

▷ A chalkboard

▷ A 5 × 8–inch index card and a pencil for each student

Procedure

1. Introduce the activity by discussing the fact that high school graduation is an important transition that means different things to different people. It is a time of leaving and letting go, and it will be more difficult for some than for others.

2. On the board write the following terms: *roles, relationships, routine, assessment of self*. Distribute the index cards. Ask each student to divide the card into four sections, labeling each section with one of the four terms and leaving space to write.

3. Have each student think about how leaving high school will change his or her roles (for example, as student, family member living at home, friend) and write one or two responses in the appropriate section of the card. Then move on to relationships, routine, and assessment of self (for example, "may not be the big athlete in a little town").

4. Have students form groups of four to share their responses for the category of roles. After several minutes, have one person from each group move to a new group, and have the newly constituted groups discuss their responses regarding relationships. Follow the same procedure for the remaining categories.

5. Discuss the Content and Personalization Questions.

Discussion

CONTENT QUESTIONS

1. Was it difficult to identify issues for these four aspects of transitions? If so, which ones were the most difficult?

2. Are these effects of a transition things you have thought about in relation to leaving high school? If not, what did you become more aware of?

PERSONALIZATION QUESTIONS

1. How do you think leaving high school will change your life?

2. How are you feeling about this transition?

3. Which aspects of the transition do you think will be easiest? Which do you think will be most difficult?

4. How have you coped with transitions in the past? What strengths can you draw from to help you with this transition?

Follow-up Activity

Invite several students who graduated last year to visit the group to discuss how their roles, relationships, routines, and assessment of self were affected by the transition out of high school. Ask them specifically to address how they dealt with these changes.

Please Pick Me

Developmental Perspective

As adolescents enter this last year of high school, relationships can sometimes become strained as they compete for scholarships, awards, and honors. It is all too easy for them to compare themselves to others and consider themselves inadequate if they are passed over or not selected as often as their peers.

Objective

▷ To examine feelings about competition and ways to deal with them

Materials

▷ A copy of the Please Pick Me–Situations (Handout 7)
  for each group of four students

▷ A marker and a sheet of newsprint for each group of four students

Procedure

1. Introduce the lesson by asking each student to think about an honor, an award, or a position in athletics or music that he or she wanted but someone else got. Elicit students' feelings about the other people, the situations, and themselves.

2. Divide students into groups of four and have each group appoint a recorder. Distribute the Please Pick Me–Situations (Handout 7) to each group. Instruct the groups to read the situations and discuss them: What feelings the teenagers had as a result of not being selected, how they felt toward the others who got what they had wanted, and what they thought about themselves and their abilities because they were passed over. Have the recorder write the group's responses on the worksheet.

3. After sufficient discussion time, distribute a marker and a sheet of newsprint to each group. Ask the groups to brainstorm ways to deal with self-put-downs, expectations, and competitive feelings, and have them list these ideas on the newsprint. Then have each group briefly summarize the results of the discussion and share their suggestions for dealing with these issues with the total group.

4. Discuss the concept of *self-talk* as a way of dealing with the disappointment of not being chosen. Use the following explanation:

> Self-talk involves giving messages to yourself to challenge the negative things you may be thinking. For example, if you weren't selected for a scholarship, you might be thinking you are dumb, others are better than you are, or you are totally worthless. To challenge this, you would ask yourself questions such as the following: "Where is the evidence that I am a totally worthless person just because I didn't get this scholarship? Does not getting this scholarship necessarily mean that I am dumb? And just because someone else got the scholarship I applied for, does it mean they are a better person, or could it just mean that someone judged their application more favorably?"

Ask students to share examples of self-talk that could have been used in the situations on the handout.

5. Discuss the Content and Personalization Questions.

Discussion

CONTENT QUESTIONS

1. Do you think the issues and feelings described in the situations in the handout are commonly experienced by students in your high school? Why or why not?

2. Which suggestions do you think would be the most helpful for dealing with feelings of inadequacy and the expectations of others?

PERSONALIZATION QUESTIONS

1. Can you personally identify with any of the situations on the handout? If you weren't selected for something you wanted, how did you deal with your own expectations and the expectations of others? Did this situation affect your relationship with peers in any way?

2. If you aren't selected for an award or a position of some sort, what does this say about you? Does it mean you are inadequate or a bad person?

3. If you aren't selected for an award or a position, do you think it will have a long-lasting negative impact on your life? Why or why not?

Follow-up Activity

Encourage students to develop effective self-talk to counteract feelings of inadequacy in competitive situations they have experienced or anticipate experiencing.

Please Pick Me

SITUATIONS–PAGE 1

Instructions: In your small group, read each situation and discuss responses to the questions. Have one person write the group's responses.

1. Kristin was sure she would be elected to National Honor Society. She had good grades, she had done a lot of community volunteer work, and she was very active in several school activities. However, she was not elected.

    How do you think Kristin felt about not being elected? _____

    How do you think she felt toward others who were elected? _____

    What might she be thinking about herself and her abilities because she didn't get elected?

    _____

2. Terrell desperately wanted to be captain of the football team. He knew the choice was between him and Mike, and Mike was selected.

    How do you think Terrell felt about not being selected? _____

    How do you think he felt toward Mike? Toward the team?_____

    What might he be thinking about himself and his abilities because he didn't get selected?

    _____

3. On graduation night, school officials were going to be awarding five 1,500-dollar scholarships. Dominic knew she would be letting her parents down if she weren't one of the five recipients. She was afraid she might not get a scholarship, even though her grades were excellent. When the recipients were announced, Dominic was not one of them.

    How do you think Dominic felt about not getting a scholarship?_____

    How do you think she felt toward the scholarship recipients? _____

    What might she be thinking about herself and her abilities because she didn't get the scholarship?

    _____

Please Pick Me

SITUATIONS–PAGE 2

4. Shiron had practiced very diligently for the last month in hopes that he would be selected for the all-state orchestra. His older brother had been first-chair bass, and even though his parents hadn't said anything, he thought they wanted him to follow in his brother's footsteps. When the all-state members were announced, Shiron was not one of them.

How do you think Shiron felt about not being selected? _____

How do you think he felt toward those who were? _____

What might he be thinking about himself and his abilities because he wasn't selected?

_____

5. Karen was one of the finalists for the Wal-Mart scholarship. She really was counting on getting it. It seemed like this year she had been passed over for everything . . . her best friend had been homecoming queen, another good friend had been senior class president, and her boyfriend had just been awarded a presidential scholarship to attend a state university. Karen's neighbor got the scholarship.

How do you think Karen felt about not getting the scholarship? _____

How do you think she felt toward her neighbor? _____

What might she be thinking about herself and her abilities because she didn't get this award?

_____

Saying Goodbye

Developmental Perspective

During mid-adolescence, relationships take on a new dimension. Beginning at about age 17, friendships are based more on compatibility and shared experiences, and friends are chosen on the basis of their contributions to relationships as well as on personality. As young people enter the last year of high school, they begin to realize that these relationships will change as they graduate and move on to the next phase of life.

Objective

▷ To identify feelings associated with leaving and letting go of relationships

Materials

▷ Five 3 × 5–inch index cards and a pencil for each student

Procedure

1. Introduce the lesson by discussing the fact that as students finish high school, their roles and relationships will change. Distribute the index cards. Ask each student to identify five people (peers, parents, relatives, teachers, and so on) with whom he or she has significant relationships and write their names, one per card.

2. For each card, have them identify the following:
   ▶ What he or she appreciates most about that person
   ▶ One or two ways he or she thinks the relationship with that person will change after graduation
   ▶ Something he or she will miss about the relationship

3. Ask students to find partners and discuss what they feel comfortable sharing relative to what they wrote on their cards.

4. Discuss the Content and Personalization Questions.

Discussion

CONTENT QUESTIONS

1. What was it like for you to think about how your relationships with these significant people will most likely change in the near future?

2. Was it difficult to think specifically about how these relationships will change? Do you think it is possible that some of them won't change?

PERSONALIZATION QUESTIONS

1. Which relationships do you think will be the most difficult for you to deal with in terms of possible changes?

2. What feelings do you have about these significant relationships changing?

3. How do you deal with these feelings?

Follow-up Activity

Encourage students to write letters to these significant people, letting them know what they appreciate about these individuals and how they anticipate that the relationships will change. Consider inviting a panel of students who graduated a year ago to address the group on this topic.

Love You, Love You Not

Developmental Perspective

Intimate friendships with both the same gender and the opposite gender increase during adolescence, with females seeking these relationships sooner than males. Intimate relationships help adolescents develop increased social sensitivity, but at the same time they can be a source of confusion and conflict.

Objective

▷ To identify feelings and issues involved in intimate relationships

Materials

▷ A copy of the Love You, Love You Not–Poem (Handout 8) for each student

▷ Paper and pencil for each student

Procedure

1. Divide students into triads. Ask each student to think of a person with whom he or she has a very close friendship, then write down three words that characterize that relationship. Have students (without revealing the names of the people) share their adjectives in their small groups. Then have them follow the same procedure for people with whom they don't have close relationships. After some discussion, ask students whether they would select words from the positive list, words from the negative list, or words from both lists to describe an intimate relationship. Discuss the fact that sometimes these relationships start out very positively but end up negatively, so there may be feelings from both lists.

2. Distribute a copy of the Love You, Love You Not–Poem (Handout 8) to each student. Ask students to read the poem, then talk in their small groups about what it means and what message it conveys about intimate relationships.

3. Discuss the Content and Personalization Questions.

Discussion

CONTENT QUESTIONS

1. What do you think the writer of this poem was trying to convey?

2. Do you think these are typical issues in relationships during adolescence?

3. What feelings were expressed in this poem?

PERSONALIZATION QUESTIONS

    1. Can you relate to the issues and feelings expressed in this poem?

    2. If so, how do you deal with these issues and feelings?

    3. What advice would you give to your peers about being involved in intimate relationships?

Follow-up Activity

Invite students to write their own poems, stories, or songs about relationship issues.

Love You, Love You Not

POEM

You make me weak.

You make me strong.

Can't you see you control it?

You play these games and base them
around everything I have feelings for

And I think you know it.

You make me hate you

But at the same time hold the power
to make me believe I love you.

I watch every single car that passes
by my house

Thinking it's you.

What a fool I am.

Look at my imaginary world.

It won't happen ever again.

You blew it one too many times, and

I need to get off your joy ride because
it's going in one big circle.

–Alex, Age 16

Parameters with Parents

Developmental Perspective

One of the major developmental tasks for adolescents is becoming emotionally independent of parents. Although most would not admit it, they fear responsibility to some extent, yet at the same time they know they can't be dependent forever. Relationships with parents may be somewhat stormy as adolescents mask their lack of confidence with defiance.

Objectives

▷ To identify issues surrounding relationships with parents

▷ To identify effective strategies for dealing with parent-teen relationships

Materials

▷ Four sheets of newsprint displayed in various parts of the room. On each sheet should be printed one of the following words: *expectations, independence, trust, influence.* (If the group is large, you may want to have two signs per word so that subgroups are no larger than five or six students.)

▷ A copy of the Parameters with Parents–Letters (Handout 9) for each small group

▷ At least one sheet of blank newsprint and a marker per group

Procedure

1. Introduce the lesson by explaining that as young people mature, relationships with parents become more complex, particularly because they are wanting more independence. The purpose of this lesson is to identify some issues in parent-teen relationships and strategies for dealing with them.

2. Divide the group into four (or more, depending on the size of the group) smaller groups, and have each group appoint a recorder. Assign each group a newsprint sign to stand beside. Give each group a copy of the Parameters with Parents–Letters (Handout 9), a sheet of blank newsprint, and a marker. Ask one student in each group to read the handout aloud. Have group members comment on the issues or themes raised in the letters. The recorder should summarize the comments on the blank newsprint.

3. Have each group address the word on their newsprint sign. Have group members discuss what this term means to them with regard to issues with parents, particularly at this stage of development. Have the recorder summarize responses. Then have the group identify at least three things they think are helpful in getting along with parents and resolving issues related to this discussion.

4. Allow time for the small groups to share results with the total group.

5. Discuss the Content and Personalization Questions.

Discussion

CONTENT QUESTIONS

1. What was your reaction to the letters written by Eric and Ann? Could you identify with the issues they raised?

2. Do you think relationship issues with parents are different at this point in your life than they were in your earlier teen years? Why or why not?

PERSONALIZATION QUESTIONS

1. How would you characterize your relationship with your parent(s) at this stage of your life? Which of the four words on the newsprint signs are the most significant ones for you with regard to your issues with your parent(s)?

2. What strategies do you find helpful in trying to resolve issues with your parent(s)?

Follow-up Activity

Suggest journal keeping or letter writing as a way of expressing feelings and trying to resolve parent-teen relationship issues.

Parameters with Parents

LETTERS—PAGE 1

Instructions: Have one member of the group read aloud these short letters written by two 18-year-olds. Comment on the themes and issues you hear reflected.

Dear Mom and Dad,

I'm sorry for how I acted tonight. There's no excuse, so I'm not even going to try to find one. I don't want to make our last summer before college hell for you. I appreciate the freedom and understanding that you've given me. I'll try to be better. I'm sorry, and I love you.

−Eric

Dear Mom,

I have been miserable for quite a while now, and I know that you have been, too. We're back in that rut again, and I don't know how to get out of it. I know you have a lot on your mind, but why don't you forget about worrying about me? I am old enough to take care of myself.

I don't think that you really trust me, or else you wouldn't wonder about me all the time. Like you said, if you don't trust me now, you never will. I don't know how to change that, but I wish I did.

I've tried to please you this year, and that's the reason I broke up with Terry. But now you don't seem happy about the fact that I am dating other guys. I just want to have fun, and I'm not planning on marriage. Why are you always trying to curtail my activities? For once it would be nice if you would just tell me to have a good time. I hate having to account for every minute, and I hate it when you flash the light when it's time to come in, like I'm some little kid. It would be nice if I could come and go when I felt like it. After all, I do have some common sense. But maybe you don't know that since you haven't given me many chances to prove it. You are the one who brought me up, and you should have some confidence that I learned something.

I'm 18. I can start taking care of myself. I'd better start this summer when you're still around, or I won't know what to do next year. Maybe you think I can't make decisions, but I've made quite a few good ones this year.

Parameters with Parents

LETTERS—PAGE 2

Next year when I'm gone I can do whatever I want, but that doesn't mean I will. I do have a sense of values, so please trust me and just allow me to make a few of my own decisions this summer and not have everything be so rigid. If I don't have a chance to do that, I won't know what to do next year when I'm on my own.

Please understand me. I love you, and we'll get along a lot better if you realize that I can't become independent all at once next fall, so please let me start now.

Love,

Ann

It's a Dilemma

Developmental Perspective

Because adolescents don't always carefully evaluate consequences before they take action, they find themselves facing dilemmas that may have practical as well as moral implications. Understanding more about possible dilemmas or difficult decisions may help them learn to think ahead regarding outcomes.

Objectives

▷ To learn more about difficult decisions

▷ To identify factors to consider in making difficult decisions

Materials

▷ Paper and pencil for each student

▷ A copy of the It's a Dilemma–Story (Handout 10) for each student

Procedure

1. Introduce the lesson by asking each student to think about the two most difficult decisions he or she has ever made and list them on a sheet of paper. Then, have students describe what it was about the decisions that made them difficult. Invite students to share this information with partners. In the total group, discuss in general which types of decisions are most difficult and what factors contribute to the difficulty (for example, decisions that have major implications for the future, decisions involving moral dilemmas or practical problems, decisions that affect others, decisions that have significant financial impact, and the like).

2. Distribute the It's a Dilemma–Story (Handout 10) to each student, explaining that it is a true story about a high school senior. Ask students to read the story and respond to the questions at the end.

3. Discuss the Content and Personalization Questions.

Discussion

CONTENT QUESTIONS

1. What makes a decision difficult?

2. What things do you need to consider in order to make a difficult decision?

PERSONALIZATION QUESTIONS

1. If you have had a difficult decision to make, have you been pleased with the outcome?

2. If you have made a difficult decision, how did you do it? What factors did you consider?

3. When you have difficult decisions to make, do you make them by yourself, or do you consult others? If you consult others, who do you turn to (for example, parents, teachers, friends, counselors)?

4. If you have had a difficult decision to make, did it involve a moral issue or was it more of a practical decision?

Follow-up Activity

Ask each student to interview an adult, a peer, and an older student about a difficult decision each has made, how the person made it, whether he or she consulted others, and whether he or she is happy with the outcome. The interviewer should use this information to write several "I learned" statements about making difficult decisions.

It's a Dilemma

STORY—PAGE 1

Name: _____ Date: _____

Instructions: Read this true story, and respond to the questions at the end.

Jason and I had been going out for over a year. As soon as we started to be sexually active I went on the pill. Then we started having major fights and kept breaking up all the time. I didn't want to have anything to do with him sexually, so I stopped taking the pill. Well, we got back together, and it didn't take long before I was pregnant. I finally got up the nerve to tell my parents, and before I really had a chance to think about how I was feeling or what I wanted to do, my mom took me for an abortion. Everything just seemed like such a blur, but I got through it and just started getting on with my life. I knew it was the best thing to do since I had just turned 18, but I tried not to think about it.

After the abortion, things were on again, off again with Jason. Sometimes I just didn't even want to see him because he could be so mean and treat me like dirt. I don't know why I put up with it, but I guess I still thought I loved him. We broke up again and I started going out with one of his friends, but then Jason started calling me and we gradually began spending more and more time together. I wasn't on the pill, and I got pregnant again.

Up until this point I had tried to put the first abortion out of my mind, but then everything started to hit me. I didn't know what to do. The relationship with Jason wasn't good. He was pretty heavy into drugs, had dropped out of school, and related to me only when he felt like it. Most of the time I was really mad at him, so I knew marriage was out of the question. Also, I had no idea what kind of father he'd be. The second option was another abortion, and I just didn't think I could do that again. So for me there were two alternatives: keep the baby or give it up for adoption.

It's a Dilemma

STORY—PAGE 2

There were days when I just tried to pretend this wasn't happening, but I knew sooner or later I would have to face reality. I felt like my mom, dad, and stepmother wanted me to have the baby and give it up for adoption or have another abortion. They kept pointing out to me how this would interfere with my plans to go to college because I'd have the extra responsibility if I kept the baby, and I'd have to get a job to support us. They were afraid the baby might have problems because Jason had been so heavy into drugs. They also were concerned that he would make my life even more miserable if there was a baby involved. I struggled with what they were saying to me. I didn't want to go through a second abortion. I also didn't think I could give the baby up for adoption. I had been adopted, and even though I think my life has been a whole lot better because I wasn't raised by a young mother who had no money or education, there was something about doing that to someone else that just bothered me. I didn't ever think much about my biological parents, but I didn't want my baby to have to wonder why I gave it up and what I was like. I just didn't know what to do.

My parents kept telling me to think this through carefully. I was only 18, and I would have this responsibility for the rest of my life. They didn't think I realized the significance of that, and maybe I didn't. I felt trapped. Regardless of the choice I made, I would always live with the consequences.

–Mia, Age 18

Is this an example of a moral decision, a practical decision, or both?_____

_____

What kind of impact will Mia's decision have on her future? _____

_____

What things do you think Mia should take into consideration in making her decision?

_____

If you are a young woman, what would you do in this situation? _____

_____

If you were Jason and Mia were your girlfriend, what would you do? _____

_____

Goals Galore

Developmental Perspective

Although the sense of time for many adolescents is still very present tense, they are entering a transitional period that necessitates goal setting. Learning the steps in a goal-setting process will give them a skill they can use now and in the future.

Objective

▷ To learn how to set and attain goals

Materials

▷ A chalkboard

▷ Paper and pencil for each student

Procedure

1. Introduce the lesson by asking students to define *goal* and to differentiate between long-term and short-term goals. Discuss the fact that a goal is an idea of something one would like to achieve and that in order to do so, one needs to identify specific objectives (small steps) to help one reach the ultimate goal. Emphasize to students that at this point in their lives, long-term goals may be things they would like to achieve within the next 1 to 5 years but that as they get older, their long-term goals may reach out 10 or 15 years.

2. Ask each student to write one short-term goal (something to achieve within the next month) and one long-term goal (something to achieve within the next year or two). Ask students to share examples, and list these on the board under two headings: *short-term goals* and *long-term goals*. Then, ask students to consider their short-term goals and identify the specific objectives needed to achieve those goals, as in this example:

   ▸ Short-term goal: To get a job within the next month

   Objective 1: Buy a newspaper and look in the help-wanted section.

   Objective 2: Analyze the job openings to see which ones you would be interested in.

   Objective 3: Go to the places that interest you and get applications.

   Objective 4: Fill out the applications and submit them.

   Objective 5: Repeat this procedure if it doesn't result in a satisfactory job.

Have students repeat this procedure with their long-term goals, as in this example:

► Long-term goal: To buy a good used car after high school graduation

Objective 1: Get a good job to make money to pay for the car.

Objective 2: Put a specific amount of money each month in a car savings account.

Objective 3: Determine the type of car you want by reading *Consumer Reports* and car magazines and talking to dealers.

Objective 4: Look for good buys in the paper or on car lots.

Objective 5: Buy the car when you have enough money to pay for the car you think is the best deal.

Explain that setting realistic timelines is also an important part of goal setting. For each objective identified, one should establish a specific deadline. For example, under the long-term goal of buying a car, a timeline for Objective 1 might be "to have a good job no later than a month from now."

3. When students have finished writing their objectives, ask them to share their results in triads. Discuss the importance of setting specific objectives as a way of both ensuring attainment of a goal and breaking down a task so it seems more manageable.

4. Discuss the Content and Personalization Questions.

Discussion

CONTENT QUESTIONS

1. What is the difference between long-term and short-term goals?

2. Why is it important to establish very specific objectives in conjunction with a goal?

3. Do you think it is more important to set goals at this stage of your life than it was several years ago? Why or why not?

4. Do you think everyone has short-term goals? If some people don't, why do you think they don't, and how do you think this affects them? Do you think everyone has long-term goals? If not, why do you think they don't, and do you think this has any impact?

PERSONALIZATION QUESTIONS

1. Do you typically establish goals for yourself? If so, are they long term, short term, or both?

2. Do you establish specific objectives and timelines to help you achieve your goals? If you don't, do you think this presents any problems for you?

3. How do you feel about your ability to achieve goals? Is there anything you'd like to change in order to be more successful? If so, what will you do and how will you do it?

Follow-up Activity

Have each student identify a short-term goal, specific objectives, and a timeline for the objectives. Provide time for students to share these with partners. Partners should help each other rework objectives if they are too vague and monitor each other's progress in achieving the objectives.

Big Decisions

Developmental Perspective

Despite the fact that they have better cognitive skills at this stage of development, adolescents can easily become overwhelmed by the number of important decisions they need to make as they prepare for a major life transition. Being aware of these major decisions is a first step in deciding among alternatives.

Objectives

▷ To distinguish between major and minor decisions

▷ To identify personal examples of major and minor decisions

Materials

▷ Paper and pencil for each student

▷ A sheet of newsprint with the following written on it:

     Whom to go with to the prom

     What subjects to take this year

     What to do after high school

     What to wear for senior pictures

     Which scholarships to apply for

     What kind of car to buy

     What to do over the weekend

     Whether or not to skip school

     Whether or not to go to the senior keg party

     Whether or not to break up with the person you have been dating all year

Procedure

1. Introduce the lesson by asking students to distinguish between major and minor decisions. Post the sheet of newsprint. Ask students to find partners and decide which decisions would be major and which would be minor.

2. Have the pairs share conclusions with the total group. Initiate discussion about what students think determines whether a decision is major or minor: Does it vary according to the individual, according to the consequences, and so on?

3. Ask students to find new partners and brainstorm examples of decisions they need to make during their senior year. Have pairs list these on paper and attempt to classify them as major decisions (MAJ) or minor decisions (MIN). Next, have each pair identify a minimum of five factors they need to consider in making major decisions. Invite sharing of examples with the total group.

4. Discuss the Content and Personalization Questions.

Discussion

CONTENT QUESTIONS

1. How do you decide whether a decision is major or minor?

2. What resources can you call on in making major and minor decisions?

3. Do you think major decisions ever become minor decisions?

PERSONALIZATION QUESTIONS

1. Are most of your decisions major or minor?

2. What feelings do you associate with making major decisions? Minor decisions?

3. When you make a major decision, do you usually make it alone, or do you consult others?

4. How do you feel about your ability to make good minor decisions? Good major decisions?

Follow-up Activity

Have students keep track of all the decisions they make during a two-week period. Ask them to classify the decisions as major or minor, identify how they arrived at their decisions, and explain how they felt about the decisions they made.

Priorities, Please

Developmental Perspective

As young people approach the end of mid-adolescence, by necessity they begin assuming more responsibility. As a result, they need to be able to establish priorities and develop good time management skills. Because they are able to think more abstractly, they can see possibilities. However, seeing possibilities can be over-whelming. It is therefore important to teach young people how to establish priorities within a list of possibilities and to manage time effectively.

Objectives

▷ To develop the ability to set priorities

▷ To develop time management skills

Materials

▷ A chalkboard

▷ A copy of the Priorities, Please–Diagrams (Handout 11) for each student

▷ Paper and pencil for each student

▷ A sheet of newsprint and a marker for each group of four students

▷ A roll of masking tape

Procedure

1. Introduce the lesson by asking each student quickly to jot down five things he or she would choose to do on a Saturday if there were no work commitments or other responsibilities. Then ask students to define the word *priority* (preceding in importance) and discuss how they decide on priorities. Ask them to prioritize their lists, numbering the first priority as 1, and so on. Invite students to share examples, and list examples of the number-1 priorities on the board.

2. Discuss the importance of setting priorities in order to accomplish goals. Ask students to find partners and share examples of times when they have established priorities in order to achieve goals. Invite sharing with the total group.

3. Distribute the Priorities, Please–Diagrams (Handout 11) to each student. Ask students to divide the first circle into pie-shaped pieces, making pie charts that represent how they spend a typical day. For example, assuming that the pie represents 24 hours, have them think about how many hours they spend in school, with family, with friends, at jobs, doing homework, participating in sports or other extracurricular activities, and so on. Then have students form groups of four to compare results.

4. Have students brainstorm on paper how they would like to spend 24 hours. After they have listed all desired activities, have them make pie charts on the second circle, designating the largest wedge for the first-priority activity and so on until they have diagrammed all activities. In their small groups, have them compare their charts.

5. Discuss the concept of time management in relation to the setting of priorities. Pose the following dilemma: Suppose that your priority is hanging out with friends, but you have a major test tomorrow. Which takes priority? Use this dilemma to stimulate discussion about how to establish priorities and manage time and whether one must consider consequences as one identifies priorities. Following this discussion, ask each small group to develop a short advice column for seniors about setting priorities and managing time. Have them write their columns on newsprint, and post them for sharing with the total group.

6. Discuss the Content and Personalization Questions.

Discussion

CONTENT QUESTIONS

1. What factors do you need to consider in setting priorities?

2. In this activity, how did your priorities (the second circle) compare with the way you actually spend your time (the first circle)? If there is a discrepancy, what accounts for this, and how do you feel about it?

PERSONALIZATION QUESTIONS

1. Considering your priorities, how well do you think you manage your time? If you don't manage it well, what prevents you from doing so? What do you think needs to change?

2. How do you think setting priorities and managing time efficiently will affect you in the next year or two? (Elicit specific examples.)

3. What is one thing you can do now to manage your time more efficiently?

Follow-up Activity

Ask students to make lists of their priorities for the coming week. In addition, ask them to keep track of how they spend their time during the coming week. At the end of the week, have them compare their lists of priorities with their records of actual time spent. Ask each student to write several "I learned" statements reflecting on this activity.

Priorities, Please

DIAGRAMS—PAGE 1

Name: _____ Date: _____

Instructions: Assume that the first circle represents a 24-hour day. Think about how you spend a typical day, and divide the circle into pie-shaped pieces according to how you spend your time. Label each section accordingly (for example, 8 hours sleeping, 6 hours in school, and so on). After you have identified how you would like to spend 24 hours, divide and label the second circle to represent these priorities.

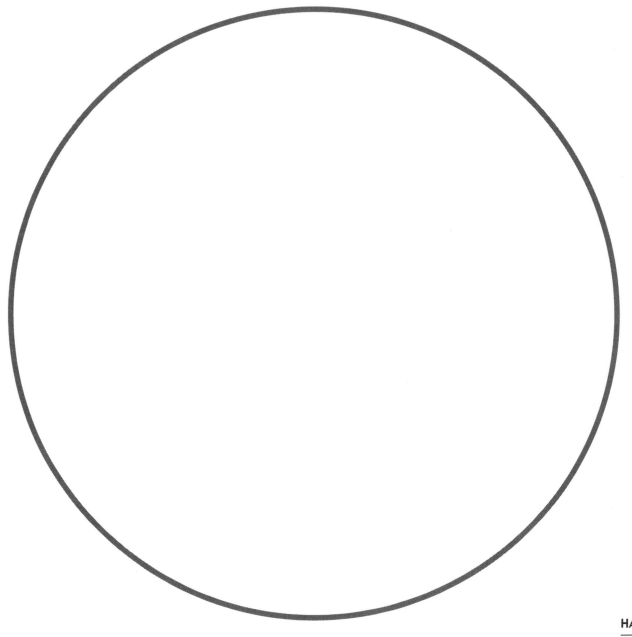

Priorities, Please

DIAGRAMS–PAGE 2

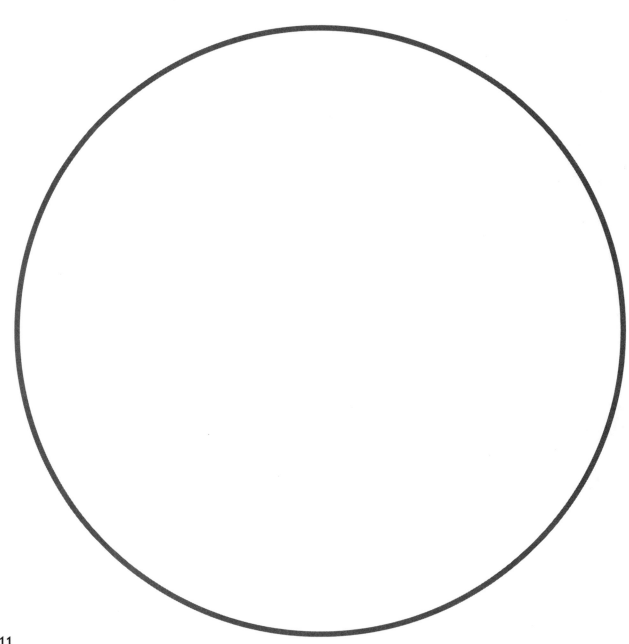

ABOUT THE AUTHOR

Ann Vernon, Ph.D., is Professor and Coordinator of Counseling in the Department of Educational Leadership, Counseling, and Postsecondary Education at the University of Northern Iowa in Cedar Falls. In addition to her university teaching, Dr. Vernon has a private counseling practice, specializing in work with children, adolescents, and their parents. She is the author of numerous articles and several books, including *Counseling Children and Adolescents; Developmental Assessment and Intervention with Children and Adolescents; Thinking, Feeling, Behaving: An Emotional Education Curriculum for Children and Adolescents;* and *What Growing Up Is All About: A Parent's Guide to Child and Adolescent Development* (coauthored with Radhi Al-Mabuk). Dr. Vernon is also Director of the Midwest Center for Rational-Emotive Behavior Therapy and conducts workshops throughout the United States and Canada on applications of REBT with children and adolescents, as well as on other topics relating to work with young people.